Advance Praise

"As a startup, our ability to ship quality products in a timely manner was crucial to our long term success. This book, containing a summary of our engineering model, presents the hard won principles and techniques that were used to deliver great software under pressure and on time."

—Frank Grossman, Jim Moskun
Founders of NuMega Technologies

"I worked at NuMega with Ed for over six years. Although we had a bunch of smart programmers, Ed brought much needed discipline to the development process. Most of what I've learned about successfully managing great software projects, I learned from Ed. This book boils down all the hard won wisdom of those years into a succinct, easy-to-read volume."

—Matt Pietrek
Co-Founder, MindReef LLC

"Like his namesake, *this* Ed Sullivan has a really big show for us. He's one of the main reasons that NuMega builds quality software—and in this book, he shares his secrets."

—Chris Sells
Director of Engineering, DevelopMentor

"Whether you work for a startup or a large company, the engineering principles and concepts described in this book can help you consistently ship great software."

—Joe Wurm, Vice President
Distributed Products Group, Compuware Corp.

UNDER PRESSURE AND TIME

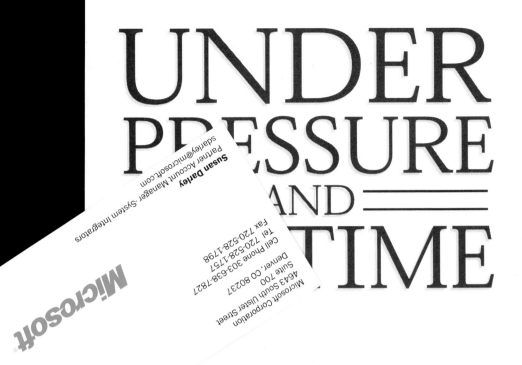

Susan Darley
Partner Account Manager, System Integrators
sdarley@microsoft.com

Microsoft Corporation
4643 South Ulster Street
Suite 700
Denver, CO 80237
Cell Phone 303-638-7827
Tel 720-528-1757
Fax 720-528-1798

Ed Sullivan
Foreword by John Robbins

PUBLISHED BY
Microsoft Press
A Division of Microsoft Corporation
One Microsoft Way
Redmond, Washington 98052-6399

Library of Congress Cataloging-in-Publication Data
Sullivan, Ed, 1962-
      Under Pressure and On Time / Ed Sullivan.
            p. cm.
      Includes index.
      ISBN 0-7356-1184-X
      1. Computer software--Development--Management.   I. Title.

   QA76.76.D47 S85   2001
   005.1'068--dc21   2001030122

Printed and bound in the United States of America.

1 2 3 4 5 6 7 8 9   MLML   6 5 4 3 2 1

Distributed in Canada by Penguin Books Canada Limited.

A CIP catalogue record for this book is available from the British Library.

Microsoft Press books are available through booksellers and distributors worldwide. For further information about international editions, contact your local Microsoft Corporation office or contact Microsoft
Press International directly at fax (425) 936-7329. Visit our Web site at mspress.microsoft.com. Send
comments to *mspinput@microsoft.com*.

Acquisitions Editor: Danielle Bird
Project Editor: Barbara Moreland

Part No. X08-04131

———◆———

To Jane, Matt, and Hannah—

All my love—always and forever.

To all NuMega employees past and present—

This book would never have been possible without you.

———◆———

CONTENTS

Foreword

Up front, I have to warn you that this book is different. While there are plenty of books available that talk about project management, *Under Pressure and On Time* talks about actually shipping software, especially from the standpoint of a startup organization. Shipping is the only thing that matters in this business, and that's what this book concentrates on. What makes this book special is that it's written by a man who didn't just get lucky shipping a single product. Ed Sullivan shipped some great products, but more importantly, he developed project managers who duplicated the same success with more products than most organizations ever dream of shipping. Growing project managers to be successful is almost impossible in this industry, but Ed did it many times, and this book gives you the same techniques he taught them.

Project management is more important than ever in the software business because everyone working in the field is on "internet-time" development schedules, which encourages teams to take shortcuts in their project management—shortcuts that lead to more slipped schedules and buggier products than ever before. This problem is especially evident in smaller software firms rushing to take advantage of a small market opening. It is also prevalent in large behemoth companies who are doing "skunk-works" development projects so they can hit that ever-elusive time-to-market window.

While you might think that project management has just not kept up with the times, the problem is much more insidious than that. No matter where you are in the world, computer science programs are not teaching real or correct project management skills; many teach none at all. Consequently, most developers are learning on their own, or they are learning from their managers who have only partially figured it out themselves. Slinging code is only 20 percent of any project, but most companies have yet to figure that out. Fortunately, what you hold in your hands will give your team the rest of the story, what you can't get anywhere else. There's no theory on project management in this book; it's simply what worked and what didn't work at a highly successful startup company.

What you will see emphasized repeatedly in this book is the team. Most company's organization charts are broken down into the fiefdom of engineering, the fiefdom of quality assurance, and, possibly, the fiefdom of documentation. The collection of individuals brought together to work on a product (in good conscience I can't call them a product team) all report to different groups with different political agendas. Consequently, most companies are set up to fail right from the beginning because of lousy organization. Ed introduced true product teams at NuMega where code developers, quality assurance developers, human factor developers, and user education developers all reported to a single project manager. Even when NuMega grew large enough to start organizing along traditional lines, Ed kept the product team concept, even when he had to fight hard to keep it. With everyone necessary to deliver a product having loyalty only to that product, NuMega was able to get past many of the artificial problems companies normally put in their way. An additional benefit is that everyone on the product team got to see how other jobs are crucial to getting a successful product out the door. That's in marked contrast to the usual us vs. them development style, especially between code developers and QA developers, that most companies practice.

Of course, getting and keeping that team together can be tough. Almost every news report about the software business these days is obliged to mention that all companies are perpetually short staffed. No amount of wishing can build a great team if you can't find the people to staff it. One thing NuMega was extraordinary at was turning up "nontraditional" developers to build the company. Ed's advice on finding and retaining great people was one of NuMega's great secrets; it allowed the company to turn in an instant and bring the right product to market at the right time. The other thing Ed did as a leader that was extraordinary for the software business was that once he got great people, he got out of the way so those people could do the job they were capable of. At times, his project managers might go four or five days without seeing or talking to him. What Ed did was let the project managers learn by making mistakes and, most importantly, he rewarded them for what they learned.

Once the great organization and great people are in place, it becomes much easier to work through the "meat" of project management. The important thing, as Ed points out in this book, is to maintain a careful balance—

managing just enough, not too much or too little. His sections on project plan-ning and project execution contain exactly what he taught his project manag-ers to do with great success. Keep in mind that it's not easy to ship successful products on time. The lessons in those sections were learned the hard way after many mistakes, plenty of teeth gnashing, and some real screaming matches!

Having participated in some of those screaming matches, I know from experience that what's in this book is worth more than you will ever pay for it. I lived everything in this book. I started out as an engineer on the BoundsChecker 3.0 team when Ed was the project manager. Eventually, I ended up being the project manager for the TrueTime and TrueCoverage product lines when Ed was the Director of Engineering at NuMega. Without the techniques Ed presents in this book, the TrueTime and TrueCoverage team could never have shipped their products as successfully as they did.

In many ways I'm jealous of you readers because you get to learn all the master's tricks without having schedule deadlines breathing down your neck. However, I'm much more fortunate because I got to learn from the master him-self. Ed helped me grow from a novice engineer to an accomplished engineer and project manager (which I never thought I would be), who now helps com-panies around the globe with their debugging and project management challenges. I can never thank Ed enough for being the best boss I ever had. Ed always joked with us that he knew enough about what we did as developers to keep us honest. Nonetheless, I still learned most of what I know about suc-cessful engineering from Ed.

When Ed first asked me to write the foreword for his book, I was abso-lutely stunned. It's such a great honor. He told me that the book was all my fault for starting him thinking about writing it and encouraging him to con-tinue. I happily plead guilty as charged! Having worked at NuMega, the most common question I get is, "How did you guys deliver so much great software at NuMega?" Now all I need to do is to point to Ed's book. I'm thrilled that everyone is getting the chance to see how one of the best project managers in the business shipped some of the most important products in the developer community time and time again.

John Robbins
Hollis, New Hampshire
January, 2001

Acknowledgments

There are so many people who contributed to the material in this book that it is truly difficult to recognize everyone, and I apologize upfront for that. However, I think it's important to recognize the key individuals and teams who helped directly or indirectly with this effort.

- John Robbins, a former teammate and co-founder of Wintellect Inc., has been encouraging me to write this book for well over two years. His endless enthusiasm and encouragement finally overwhelmed me. Thanks for your friendship and faith in me.

- My editorial and review team: Barbara Moreland and Danielle Bird of Microsoft Press, and Gabrielle Nonast and Nancy Depper of Online Training Solutions, Inc. I'd also like to thank Chris Sells of DevelopMentor for his review and comments. They did a terrific job in molding the content for this book and contributed significantly every step of the way.

- Frank Grossman and Jim Moskun, co-founders of NuMega Technologies, Inc. They taught me the theory of great software development and let me practice the art at their company. I'll always be grateful.

- The BoundsChecker 3.0, 4.0, and 5.0 development teams. The majority of the material in this book is based on your accomplishments. You guys are the best development teams I've ever known. And please stop chanting "Ed" at the movies.

- Bob O'Brien, NuMega's Public Relations Manager, and Clyde Hakim, NuMega's Marketing Communications Manager. You constantly put the spotlight on our efforts and made us look far better than we really were. You, and the rest of our marketing team, deserve as much credit as anyone else.

- My mother and father, Ed and Laura Sullivan, who taught me about life and everything that is important.

- My wife Jane, son Matthew, and daughter Hannah, who gave me the nights and weekends to work on this effort. Your enthusiasm and encouragement kept me going when I needed it the most. You are precious to me and I thank God for you every night. And yes, it's finally done!

INTRODUCTION

I joined NuMega Technologies, Inc. in the summer of 1994. I was both the development manager and the product-marketing manager of BoundsChecker, a software error detection product for Windows. At the time, NuMega employed only 14 people. In addition to the two founders, there were three engineers, a COO, four sales people, one office administrator, one shipping clerk, three support engineers, and a marketing communications manager. We were a small company—a start-up by any other name. Each person performed many jobs and had many responsibilities. Yet even though we were small, we had big plans and high hopes for the future. We were committed to building great software and wanted to assemble an elite engineering team to build the world's best development tools.

Four years later, thanks to the care and feeding of the founders and a top-notch management team, the company had grown to over 150 people. I grew with the company as well, ultimately serving as its Director of Engineering. In those first four years, we shipped six major releases of our franchise products, BoundsChecker and SoftICE, acquired two new products, and created four new products internally. Almost all of these products had been shipped within their target dates. Revenue grew rapidly and we were very profitable. In fact, our products were so well received, they were honored with the following industry awards:

2000

◆ **DevPartner® for Visual Basic** wins "Best component or utility for ensuring software quality," awarded by *Vbxtra*.

◆ **BoundsChecker® VC++ Edition** wins "Riding the Crest Award" in the "Best Selling Testing and Debugging Tool" category, awarded by *Programmer's Paradise*.

- **CodeReview™ 6.1** wins VBPJ "Reader's Choice" award.

- **FailSafe™ 5.21** wins VBPJ "Reader's Choice" merit award.

1999

- **DevPartner Studio** receives Jolt Cola "Award for Product Excellence" from *Software Development Magazine*.

- Software Development 5 Star rating for **DevPartner Studio**.

- *Java Developer's Journal* "JDJ World Class Award" given to **DevPartner for Java™**.

- VBPJ "Reader's Choice" award given to **SmartCheck® 6.01**.

- **CodeReview 6.1** wins VBPJ "Reader's Choice" award.

- **DevPartner 6.1 for Visual Basic** receives VBPJ "Reader's Choice" merit award.

- VBPJ "Reader's Choice" merit award goes to **TrueTime®**.

1998

- **DevPartner for Visual Basic** receives "Thunderbolt" award from *Vbxtras*.

- **SmartCheck** and **TrueTime** receive "Editor's Choice" from *Visual Basic Programmer's Journal*.

- **SmartCheck** and **TrueTime** receive "Reader's Choice" award from *Visual Basic Programmer's Journal*.

- **DevPartner for Visual Basic** receives Jolt Cola "Productivity Award" from *Software Development*.

1997

- **BoundsChecker®** is the first-ever inductee into the *Software Development* "Jolt Hall of Fame." It is cited for winning multiple awards through consistent performance.

- **TrueTime® Visual Basic Edition** wins *BYTE*'s Comdex "Best of Show."

- **SmartCheck®** earns "Analyst Choice" from *PC Week.*
- **BoundsChecker** receives the 1997 "Reader's Choice" award from *Visual Basic Programmer's Journal* for the second year in a row.

1996

- **CodeReview™** receives the 1996 "Star Tech" award from *Windows Tech Journal* as one of 1996's most significant software development tools.
- **BoundsChecker** receives *PC Magazine's* "Editors Choice" award in an extensive competitive review.
- **BoundsChecker** for Windows NT receives *PC Magazine's* "Technical Excellence Award for Best Development Tool" for 1996.
- **BoundsChecker** receives a Jolt Cola "Productivity Award for Product Excellence" at the Software Development West '96 Conference.
- **BoundsChecker** receives the 1996 "Reader's Choice" award from *Visual Basic Programmers Journal*.

1995

- **BoundsChecker** receives the "Star Tech" award from *Windows Tech Journal* as one of 1995's most significant software development tools.
- **BoundsChecker for Windows NT** receives the Jolt Cola "Award for Product Excellence" at the Software Development West '95 Conference.

1994

- **BoundsChecker for Windows** receives the Jolt Cola "Award for Product Excellence" at the Software Development '94 Conference.

Sounds great, right? But we faced the same problems as any other software development team: conflicting goals, schedule pressure, insufficient resources, burnout, and communication problems, just to name a few. But we had to ship quality software in a timely manner or face the risk of going out of business.

The biggest obstacle our engineering team overcame is also the most widespread problem in the software industry today—the ineffective management of software teams and projects. Startup companies in particular face this problem every day and must solve it or go bankrupt. At NuMega Technologies, our ability to solve this problem is one of the most important reasons why we succeeded.

The purpose of this book is to share with you the hard-won principles, processes, and techniques for developing award-winning commercial software in a growing, startup environment. I'll cover the most critical and fundamental principles we used to get a quality release out the door. I don't get academic or talk about the hundreds of things you might want to try. I'll tell you what's actually been successfully used in a commercial startup environment. I'll also tell you about my experiences at NuMega—how we grew our engineering team and developed products at a startup company.

I believe that the startup environment is not much different from most small to medium development projects (30 people or fewer). Whether you are in a small company or a large company, an ISV or an IT shop, and whether you're an Assembler Guru or a Web developer, you need to ship great software on time. You're under pressure. You deal with the same problems. You want to have the same success. And after all, when was the last time you and your team didn't face conflicting goals, scheduling issues, insufficient resources, and all the other joys of a typical software development life cycle?

Please note that this book is not an exhaustive treatment of any one subject. There are other books available for the deep, detailed treatment of specific subjects like recruiting, release engineering, quality assurance, human factors, and so on. But as I am sure you have discovered, there is seldom time to perform any single step exhaustively in the development cycle, so you need to know the difference between what you must have and what you can do without. You want to master the essentials and not worry about the superfluous. If there are shortcuts, take them. If there's no other way but the long way, do that, too.

On the other hand, this book is not a survey of different opinions about how something should be done. You won't find a critique of all the different strategies for performing a particular task. Instead, I'll share with you a set of proven techniques that we actually used and show you how we tied them together into a fast and effective path through a development cycle. Although there are some terrific ideas that we could have adopted, my intention is to focus on the techniques we actually used.

How to Use This Book

Although I'm not suggesting that the information in this book will fit every software group or work for every software company, I do believe that much of the information will be helpful to a wide range of organizations and projects. My hope is that you'll customize and adapt as much of the information as possible for your own projects. This is not the only way to build software, but it is one proven and successful way.

Who Should Read This Book

You should read this book if you are (or hope to be) in a leadership position for a software engineering project. This includes:

- Senior engineering management (VPs, directors, group managers)
- Development managers
- Project leaders
- Development leads
- Architects
- Program managers
- Tech writing managers
- Tech writing leads
- Quality managers
- Quality leads
- Usability managers
- Usability leads
- Release managers
- Release engineering leads

You should also read this book if you are one of the individual contributors to a development team. This book describes how the entire team—not just management or leads—needs to think about software development. It's important that the entire team acts as a unit, adopting the same concepts, attitudes, beliefs, and culture.

ORGANIZATION

This book is divided into three parts. Each part describes one critical aspect of software engineering management.

Part I: People, Organization, and Methods

Before you start planning your project or writing software, you must make sure you have the fundamentals in place. You need the right people, the right organizational structure, and the right processes in place to be effective. Without these in place, your efforts to stay on schedule will be frustrated—and can ultimately fall apart—as the project accelerates and the pressure increases. In Part I, I explain the fundamental needs of any fast-paced project, including:

- *People*   Who you need, how to find them, and how to keep them.
- *Organization*   What the basic roles and responsibilities are for each team member.
- *Tools*   What the key development tools are, and how to use them.
- *Quality*   How to perform quality assurance in parallel with its development.
- *Release engineering*   How to keep your project integrated and usable throughout the development cycle.

Part II: Project Definition and Planning

If you really want to ship software on time, then you must understand what you want to build and how you are going to build it—before you build it. Even the most talented people need to have a basic idea of what they are trying to do, the technology they are going to use, and what the product should look like when it's done. Accordingly, you need to define the following:

- The basic requirements of the project.

- The technology of the project.

- The usage model of the project.

With these in place you can create a schedule that will balance the project's goals against the staff and talent you have. You can be assured—with some degree of certainty—that you have a realistic schedule for what you want to build.

These four topics—requirements, technology, usability, and schedule—are intimately related and must be handled simultaneously if you want to manage a successful project. Without them, you are guessing, assuming, or ignoring key elements of your project, thereby introducing unacceptable risks that often result in problems and large, unanticipated slips in the schedule. Remember, many of the biggest mistakes are made in the first few weeks of the project—during the planning phase.

Part III: Project Execution

Once your planning is complete, you will be ready to build the product. With good people, solid processes, and good planning in place, you have an excellent chance of making your date. But you need to make sure you don't get lost as you head for home.

Part III is focused on the execution models that drive the day-to-day development of the product. The following topics are covered:

- *Execution*   How to keep the project on track by finding and fixing problems early.

- *Beta testing*   How to get real-world feedback from a beta program and augment your testing efforts at the same time.

- *Release candidates*   How to manage the final stage of the project and make sure it's ready to ship.

- *Project closure*   What it is, why it's needed, and how to do it.

ADDITIONAL FEATURES

At the end of each chapter, I address the common questions and problems that often are raised when applying the material. Almost all of these questions and problems come from real-world experience, so I hope the solutions will help you in your real-world situations.

Also, throughout the book there are "Back at Work" sidebars that highlight how we at NuMega applied a specific principle or concept. These sidebars allow me to share some of the more interesting stories, comments, and anecdotes that make software development so much fun.

FEEDBACK

I'd like to hear your thoughts and comments on the material presented in this book. I'd also like to hear about your own hard-won lessons and how you've been able to deliver your software products on time. Please contact me at *eds_books@hotmail.com*.

PART I

PEOPLE, ORGANIZATION, AND METHODS

1

Great People and How to Find Them

G reat people make great software. They define the requirements, create the technology, and stick to the schedule. They test, document, and support the product. The ideas they have, the decisions they make, and the effort, professionalism, and excitement they put into their work make or break the development effort. Because the people who work on the project have the biggest impact on its success or failure, it is essential to hire the most qualified people possible.

Although it's true that everyone wants to hire great people, project teams often accept less qualified candidates than they should. The inability to find candidates or to discern talent can combine with the pressure to ship the product and overwhelm even the best of intentions. If you are unable to solve these problems, you'll have a mediocre team at best and an under-performing one at worst. You can't assume that talented people will just come to you—not regularly, anyway. Instead, you need a firm, organization-wide commitment to getting and keeping the most qualified people possible. This commitment must encompass three key activities: recruiting, interviewing, and retention.

In this chapter and the following chapter, I'll discuss some of the best techniques for finding, selecting, and keeping talented people. I'll also cover how these activities, like software development itself, require planning, discipline, and execution.

DEFINING "GREAT"

Before you set out to find great candidates, you must be sure about what you are looking for. If you can't describe what you want, how are you ever going to know if you've found it? What are the attributes that separate great developers, awesome technical writers, and superstar quality engineers from the not so great? There are obviously many different attributes and many different opinions, but I've boiled it down to six basic attributes.

EXPERTISE

Each potential candidate must have an area of expertise. If you're looking for a developer, he or she needs to have a specific area of technical expertise. If you need a technical writer, the candidate should have expertise in the creation of educational material. If you're hiring a quality engineer, that person's experience should be in automation and testing techniques.

I'm not talking competence here—I'm really talking about expertise. The candidate must have mastery or near mastery of a subject that is pertinent to the project's needs. He or she should be able to give an impromptu talk about his or her subject at any time and show a deep level of understanding about what was done and how it was accomplished. A developer, for example, could talk about any technical knowledge he or she possesses that matches the requirements of the position you have open. Some possible topics include:

◆ C++ and object oriented design

◆ Creating COM controls

◆ MFC and user interface development

◆ Assembler and Windows internals

◆ Device driver development

◆ Networking protocol development

◆ Performance tuning

Why is an area of expertise so important? First, if this person has been able to master at least one subject, he or she likely has the skills to master other subjects as they emerge. Technology changes quickly, and the ability to educate oneself and to comprehend significant complexity will be a critical skill.

Second, in high-powered development teams, it's important that there be mutual respect between the team members, and respect is often based on knowledge and ability. As you create a highly talented team, it's very important that each person has one or more areas of expertise in which he or she can contribute as much or more than anyone else.

Does this mean that every developer must have a PhD in computer science and 20 years of experience in software development? No, that's not the idea. But if you've decided to hire a junior developer for support and maintenance, you want to make sure he or she will have the expertise to excel in the position—not just get by.

When you interview the candidate, you should work hard to find and verify that person's area of expertise and make sure it complements your immediate or expected needs. (I'll talk more about interviewing later.)

COMMITMENT

Commitment is another important factor when looking for the most qualified people. In virtually any development project, there will be times when the project isn't going well. You never know what the problems will be ahead of time—your competitor announces their product first, a key developer has health problems, the performance of the product is pitifully slow—but it will be your people's commitment to the project and their belief in what they are doing that will carry the project through. They will show dedication to their tasks and won't stop working and helping until the project is complete. The most committed people see a project through to the end, and they are willing to make the sacrifices necessary to bring about success.

ATTITUDE

Great people often have a great attitude and great energy. They are positive and not cynical; they dwell on the good and not on the bad. They are upbeat

---

Back at Work

NuMega's release of BoundsChecker 4.0 is an excellent example of what a committed and motivated team can do. It was December 1995, the Internet revolution was just beginning, and Bill Gates had just announced Microsoft's new plans for the Internet. On December 8, the day after the announcement, we got a call from Microsoft asking if we could support their Sweeper SDK and new Internet initiatives. If so, we could do joint press releases and demos at the upcoming Software Development West show in early March. The offer was great for a startup company, but we had less than three months to get this work done, we were in the middle of a release, we had a very small team, and we were just entering the holiday season.

What was the team's response? It was awesome. Everyone recognized the opportunity and knew we needed to take the risk. Starting that afternoon, we put together an updated development plan based on the new facts that we had before us. Of course it wasn't perfect, and there were a lot of unknowns, but we had the germ of a plan, and we worked together. During the next three months, the team was committed to doing whatever was needed to get the job done. And yes, we made it, and it was a great show!

---

and encouraging and can adapt quickly. Find these people. Get them on your team. They will be essential in steering the morale of the team during the development cycle, particularly during the difficult times. Their enthusiasm will be infectious and will help define the spirit of the team.

BEHAVIOR

You want people who have a bias for action, the kind of people who go out of their way to make things happen. Being smart and positive during the development cycle is wonderful, but it's the bias for action that sets great people apart. This type of person will go out of his or her way to accept more responsibility, to fix a few extra bugs, or to send an e-mail message to keep communication flowing and see what other teams are up to. You want people who are action-oriented and who go the extra mile.

TEAM SKILLS

Software development requires a team of people who share ideas, opinions, and skills. It's being challenged and responding to that challenge that refines ideas. It's one person helping or encouraging another. It's the feeling that no one is finished until the project is finished. It's the true enjoyment and fun of working together on something great. Teams develop software. If you don't have a great team, you won't develop great software.

Because it's critical to have people who can work well with others, it's important to maintain the team's cohesion. Don't let anything get in the way of that. If a technical superstar can't work with others, his or her value to the team is seriously diminished. In the worst cases, this type of person can ruin the team itself. The health of the team must come first.

THIRST FOR KNOWLEDGE

You are looking for people who have a thirst for knowledge, people who are continually educating themselves and finding new and interesting ways to use technology. They are interested in the latest trends and are knowledgeable about the industry they work in; they will not let themselves become obsolete. They have a good understanding of what has happened with software in the past, what is happening now, and what could happen in the future. Having people like this on your team is a tremendous asset when making critical decisions that will have long-range impacts on your projects. It will also allow your team to move quickly and more easily to new technologies, tools, or methods. You can't overestimate the value of a team that can keep up with the pace of change in the industry.

GREAT PEOPLE VS. PERFECT PEOPLE

Although you are looking for the most qualified people, you must remember that no one is perfect. You're looking for the people who measure well in all the areas I've just discussed, but it's not practical to think that you'll find candidates who are perfect in every way.

For example, if a person has great technical expertise, has shown great commitment to his project, works well in a team, and reads everything he can get his hands on, but is not overly upbeat and positive, would this person be right for the team? Probably—as long as there are no signs of cynicism or other attitude problems. It's a good bet he'd make a fine addition to the team.

Another important factor is a candidate's ability to grow. Look for growth potential in a person: his or her raw talents, work ethic, and attitude. What the candidate knows on that first day might not be as important as what he or she will know and will be able to do in three months, six months, and a year. Be sure to look for growth potential when a candidate is not as advanced as the others on your team. Don't be afraid to bring on budding talent and grow it.

Back at Work

At NuMega, we often brought people on board based on their desire and ability to learn. We recognized that if people had the fire in the belly and could teach themselves technology, then they had two of the most important skills for future technical success. If we found these attributes in junior candidates, we hired them. We placed them into junior engineering roles, technical support, or QA (quality assurance)—wherever we needed help and had a good match for their skills. A candidate might not know as much as your other employees, but he or she might be able to pick things up quickly and could even surpass others in time.

THE IMPACT OF A SINGLE BAD CHOICE

The impact of hiring a poor candidate can often be very significant. Let's look at some of the major problems that can happen when you make a bad hiring decision.

♦ *Inability to adequately complete assignments*   Assuming there are no extenuating circumstances, someone probably hasn't done a thorough enough job of evaluating the new employee's expertise for the job. This candidate has been hired for a job that he or she is not qualified for.

♦ *Isolation from the core of the team*   In high-powered teams, it is very important that each person carry his or her own weight. If an employee is unable to perform the work required, he or she can often become isolated from the team. For example, people will often not seek out the opinions of, ask for help from, or respect the judgment of a person who is clearly an under-performer. People will feel that they are carrying this person "on their back" and are being unfairly punished for his or her inability to contribute. If you have more than one under-performer you may start to develop factions, which can be a breeding ground for politics and even larger discontent. Don't let this happen on your team. Everyone needs to contribute in some important way for the team to operate well.

♦ *Lower team morale and spirit*   The saying "one bad apple can ruin the bunch" has merit. If one member of the team is impossible to work with, morale and team spirit can plummet. If people don't enjoy working together, the benefits of the team are not fully realized. You need to check that all candidates—especially those who would be in leadership roles—are a good fit in the team.

♦ *Falling behind as technology moves forward*   The ability to respond to changes in the industry is very important for your team's overall success. For example, if you decide that your typical two-tier client/server application strategy needs to be upgraded to a web-oriented three-tier strategy, but some of your team members can't upgrade their skills quickly enough, you'll lose time and potentially some interesting opportunities as well.

THE FINANCIAL IMPACT

Now let's look at the financial impact of making a bad hiring decision. The following is an example of the one-year and two-year payouts for a single developer:

$90,000	Salary
$5,000	Sign-on bonus
$20,000	Recruiting fee
$30,000	Social Security, benefits, education
$145,000	First year cost
$275,000	First and second year cost (includes a small raise, no bonus)

Hey, that's a lot of money! And that's only one person. Because labor is often the single largest expense on software projects, the question must be asked: Shouldn't you spend the same amount of time and energy evaluating new candidates as you do critical new technologies or development tools?

In both cases, you want to make sure you make the right selection for the money you're going to spend and the dependency you're going to create. You want to make sure your needs are met now and in the future. And you want to make sure that your selection is dependable and easy to work with. Clearly, you should evaluate your new employee with at least as much care as you use when you choose your mechanical tools. You'll be just as dependent on him or her as you are on the technology.

THE IMPACT OF POOR STAFFING OVER TIME

Thus far, I've concentrated on the impact of making a single poor hiring decision. Although one mistake is certainly a disappointment, it can be overcome, and it's not usually fatal to a project.

What is much more difficult to overcome is a period of bad staffing decisions that causes you to build a team composed of poor and mediocre performers. The following are some of the most typical problems created by a series of bad hiring choices:

◆   *An expectation of low performance*   With poor teams, low performance is the norm. It's harder to put together a string of major successes, the occasional wins are short-lived, and there is often a regression back to the "same old way it has always been." When they get off course, poor teams struggle because they have difficulty recognizing their problems and don't usually make changes quickly and decisively.

◆   *Inattention to detail and quality*   Poor teams often produce sloppy software. There's no commitment to or passion for doing the best one can and no desire to create a solid product that delights the user. Poor teams don't take a little extra time at night or at lunch to make minor improvements to the performance, to do a little more testing, or to rewrite a paragraph in the documentation. The lack of these little things adds up over time and significantly diminishes the product.

◆   *Late products*   Poor teams have a very hard time planning and scheduling product releases. They often do not understand the complexity of the technology they are working with, are unable to anticipate the problems that might arise, and become unwilling to make the sacrifices needed to get things done on time. I'm not suggesting that if a project is late, you have a poor team. There can be many reasons for schedule slips. But I am suggesting that poor teams will continually exhibit these traits, and that these problems are often the result of poor hiring decisions.

FINDING AND ATTRACTING GREAT CANDIDATES

You now need to find great candidates and get their résumés in your hands. There are nine basic techniques or channels for finding candidates. At NuMega, we used almost all of them. We never knew where a good candidate would come from, so we were prepared to use whatever mechanism we had at our disposal. Each technique has advantages and disadvantages, and some work much better than others—especially for startups. Table 1, on the following page, is a summary of what we found.

TABLE 1-1   CHANNELS FOR FINDING NEW EMPLOYEES

Channel	Value or Potential	Effort Required	Good for Startups?
Recruiting Web sites	High	Medium	Yes
Company's Web site	High	Medium	Yes
Referrals	High	Medium	Yes
Professional recruiters	Medium	Medium	Yes
Colleges	Medium	Medium	Yes
Ads and job fairs	Low	Low	No
Trade shows	Low	Low	No
Cold calling/targeting	Low	High	No
Exceptional events	Low	Medium	No

Reviewing each one of these channels in more depth will help you decide what might work best for you.

RECRUITING WEB SITES

The Internet is probably the most important way to recruit people today. As you know, the Internet's biggest advantage is its enormous worldwide reach and its ability to work for you around the clock. In addition to the typical job posting in newsgroups, one of the best ways to use the Internet is to take advantage of the online career and job sites. I strongly encourage you to investigate these sites; they can be an exceptional way to reach technical talent. Two good recruiting Web sites are *www.monster.com* and *www.hotjobs.com*.

The general idea is simple: You, as the employer, post your job descriptions on the Web site, and potential candidates search the listings to find job opportunities. To make this work, you need to have rock-solid job descriptions. The Web sites typically allow only a couple of paragraphs in which you can describe the opportunity you have available, so make sure the description sells the position, technology, and work environment. If you don't do it well, you're unlikely to get any hits at all—there's just too much to choose from today.

YOUR WEB SITE

Your company's Web site is also critical. Although it's common for most employers to describe their job opportunities there, most don't appreciate how important their sites are to potential candidates. It needs to have the ability to draw prospects in as well as the ability to sell your organization.

Drawing Candidates In

Most small or emerging companies don't have the name recognition or visibility to draw potential candidates to their sites, so it's unlikely that you'll have a lot of success attracting people to your company with your Web site alone. However, if you're a larger or well-known company, you should leverage this advantage. It's quite common for job seekers to visit the Web sites of companies that they have heard about or know are doing well.

As your company grows and becomes more visible, you'll see more traffic from potential candidates. Be ready. If your company is already well-known, be sure to take advantage of your visibility and communicate your employment opportunities to everyone who visits your Web site.

Selling Your Opportunities

Regardless of your company's ability to draw people to its Web site, you need to have excellent material detailing your employment opportunities posted there. No matter how the potential candidate came to know about your company (recruiter, ads, referrals, and the like), it's now up to your Web site to really sell the position and the company. You want them to get a very positive and lasting impression from what they see. Is the site professionally done? Is it clear, accurate, fun, interesting, and educational? Don't simply list the job descriptions—show people why it's great to work at your company.

Almost all good candidates will check out the company's Web site before the interview. Even if your company is small and you're strapped for resources and time, it is important that you make a strong outward statement to potential candidates about your company and the opportunities you have available. The next page lists some of the critical tasks your site needs to accomplish.

- Provide clear and accurate job descriptions.
  - Describe the positions available.
  - Describe the technology involved.
  - State the years of experience required.

- Provide interesting project or product descriptions.
  - Explain what the software can do.
  - Explain why the products are important to the organization or company.
  - Detail what essential skills employees learn by working on this project.
  - Include a photo of the development team to make your team approachable.

- Provide information about the company's background and successes.
  - State the company's purpose and vision for the future.
  - State how long the company has been in business.
  - State whether the company is public or private.
  - State whether the company is venture financed.
  - State what the company's successes have been.
  - Include one of the company's recent press releases.
  - Include photos of the company's building, interior, café, and amenities.

- Describe the company's benefits program.
  - Describe the standard benefits package.
  - Detail exceptional perks that make your benefits different or better.

- Describe the work environment.
  - State whether the dress is formal or casual.
  - State whether flextime is available.
  - State whether recreation activities are available.
  - State whether there are special social activities at work.

REFERRALS

Employee referrals are absolutely essential, especially for startups and small companies. Referral programs encourage current employees to recruit former co-workers, friends, or acquaintances. Instead of paying a high-priced recruiting fee to a professional recruiter, a portion of the recruiting fee goes to the employee. It's a great idea and can work really well if you put the necessary time and energy into it.

A referral program is based on a very simple concept: High-quality people generally know or have developed a network of high-quality associates. The network often crosses disciplines—software developers know tech writers, architects know managers, and so on. Another great feature of a referral program is that referrers put their own credibility on the line and vouch for the person they are referring to you by stating their willingness to work with that person again.

In addition to being a great recruiting technique, employee referrals have many other benefits. If you have a high-quality team to begin with and use a referral program, you greatly increase your chances of staffing the team with other great people. In addition, people tend to refer people they would like to work with again. In fact, a person who refers another is generally interested in seeing that person succeed and often goes out of his or her way to make sure things are going well.

Most startup and small companies grow very quickly through referrals. It's the cheapest, simplest, and most sure-fire way of recruiting quality candidates. One warning, however: Small companies can easily become too dependent on referrals. After a period of time, referrals slow down or even dry up as all contacts have been tried. Don't rely too heavily on it, or on any one or two recruiting techniques.

Back at Work

At NuMega, during our first three years, we found that 40 percent of our candidates came in through referrals. The chain of referrals grew quite long and intricate, and it was fun to track the "begats" trail. For example, we started with Matt, who begat John, who begat Bernie, who begat Mary Lou. It was quite easy to see the power of referrals when they were all mapped out.

Referral programs work best when you put some effort into them. Hunting down past colleagues is not always the first thing on employees' minds. Regular internal communication (meetings, posters, e-mail) and strong monetary incentives are required to make the program work. Give out referral bonuses at company meetings. Make sure new employees are aware of the program; make it part of your new employee training. Have recruiters follow up with new employees a few weeks after they've started working to see if they know of any potential candidates. Referrals work, but you need to make them a priority.

PROFESSIONAL RECRUITING FIRMS

Professional recruiting firms are one of the most traditional ways of recruiting people. These firms work by taking the description of the position you have available and the qualifications you are looking for and matching them with qualified applicants. The recruiter then sends you the résumés of people who meet your needs. If you hire an applicant that the firm referred to you, you generally pay 15 percent to 25 percent of the person's first year salary to the recruiting firm as a finder's fee.

One of the best ways to use professional recruiting firms is to develop a strong relationship with them. If you can demonstrate that you're willing to take the time to work with them, describe the opportunities, and provide feedback, you'll get better results. You'll get even better results if you agree to limit the number of recruiting firms you use, pay a high premium per candidate, and show that you have many positions to fill. This provides a real incentive for the recruiting firm and can often result in your getting first crack at the best candidates they find.

The advantages of recruiting firms are easy to see. You are paying someone else to find people to meet your needs. If you have a great recruiting firm and can afford their premium, everyone benefits. However, great recruiting firms are few and far between. In many cases, the résumés you receive from these firms are not screened well, and the recruiter provides little information about the candidate. You're still largely on your own.

COLLEGES

Recruiting at colleges is another excellent means of building a portion of your staff. At NuMega, we didn't have the resources to mount a full-blown, nationwide talent search. Instead, we identified key schools in the area and developed relationships with people there, such as deans, computer science professors, and placement officers. Once we had done this legwork, we volunteered to talk about our company, the industry, and what we were doing. As this relationship grew over time, the schools often referred high-quality seniors to us for full-time work, and we also received referrals for part-time and summer employees.

ADS AND JOB FAIRS

Advertisements and job fairs are perhaps the oldest of the recruiting techniques. But newspaper ads are very expensive, and while they tend to draw a lot of résumés, often many are from unqualified candidates. Most of the time, good people don't use ads or job fairs for employment—they tend to have their own network of people. That's why referrals are so effective. Although you might be able to find a diamond in the rough through an ad or a job fair, be prepared to dig through a stack of résumés that were sent "just in case."

TRADE SHOWS

Recruiting at trade shows can be effective, but only if you have very specialized needs and are attending the corresponding specialized show. In general, people attending trade shows attend on their company's good will and are more interested in learning than in looking for new jobs. Nevertheless, take every opportunity to sell your company or organization. If you have a booth, be sure to have flyers and information on opportunities for potential candidates.

COLD CALLING / TARGETING

Let's be truthful—most of the people you want on your team have a job already and are probably not looking for a new one. To address this issue, some companies hire recruiters who use cold calling or targeting. They identify specific companies who share a similar set of staffing needs and try to find discouraged or unhappy employees who are interested in talking about a new position. Cold calling and targeting are often used when a company is having financial difficulties or has recently been acquired.

Cold calling and targeting won't be successful, however, if the employees who are being called are happy, motivated, and well paid. In fact, most of the time, they will simply refuse to talk to the caller. This knowledge is your best defense should your organization be targeted. Just remember this general rule: If you can't keep your employees happy, someone else will.

EXCEPTIONAL EVENTS

Exceptional events include company closings and lay-offs of entire teams or departments. When this occurs, you need to move very quickly. Most companies that go through these difficulties set up employment and recruitment programs for the affected employees. Because these are relatively rare events, they are not a good way to build a staffing program. However, if you're lucky, you can sometimes get good people, often from the same team, working for you quickly.

WHICH TECHNIQUE IS BEST?

Now that I've covered the nine ways of finding résumés, your next question might be, "Which one is best?" or "Which one should I use?" Startups tend to use the Internet and referrals because they are cheaper and simpler, and most effective. You can build an organization of people using just these two techniques. The other techniques are not as popular or effective because of the time, money, and effort required.

However, because superstars and high-quality candidates are so important, and because they can be found through all channels, you should work all the channels described above. Just make sure you're working the most productive ones first.

The bottom line: You must have continual and dedicated recruiting efforts that excel in the critical areas mentioned above. Recruiting is endless; it never stops. Unless you're in a long-term hiring freeze, you must assume you're going to have some turnover and you'll need to replace those employees well as hire new people.

COMMON PROBLEMS AND SOLUTIONS

Finding quality people is probably the most difficult staffing problem today. When your staffing needs are falling behind, there is often terrific pressure to "just hire someone—anyone—who can help out." Although this move will appear to solve short-term problems by allowing you to get some work done, it is a very risky approach. Each new person will initially be a drag on the overall effectiveness of the team.

In addition, if you make a poor hiring decision, you're likely to suffer from the problems described in this chapter. Quality people will recognize a quality organization and will want to work with the best. Don't dilute your team—it might affect your future ability to recruit.

But what should you do about your resource crunch? Here's some ways to get around the problem:

- *Hire contractors*   Contractors can be effectively used to fill in gaps in the labor lines and are best when used to crank out work that is not critical or unique to your project. Even if the work is below their skill set, it still makes sense to use them to help the project move forward. Using contractors also allows your people to work on the more critical and interesting parts of the project. Contractors are temporary and so can be let go easily once the work is complete or if there are signs of incompatibility with the team.

- *Overtime*   Working overtime is another way to get the job done without sacrificing the overall quality level of the team. I'll discuss how to approach overtime in Chapter 12.

- *Remove or delay feature implementation*   Sacrificing functionality should also be considered. If there's just too much work to be done and overtime and contractors can't help, the project's schedule and feature list might be out of balance. Certainly adding more people who are less qualified will not help the situation and will probably make things worse.

- *Crank up the recruiting effort*   Perhaps the lack of quality candidates is a sign that your recruiting effort isn't very effective. Why let poor quality candidates enter into the organization, thereby creating more problems, when you really need to fix the recruiting effort?

Résumés, Interviewing, and Retention

Although a team is built one person at a time, the building process is a group effort that requires deliberate and careful action. This chapter covers the fundamentals of building a team—reviewing résumés, interviewing candidates, hiring staff, and keeping the team happy.

The ability to discern a good candidate from a bad candidate by looking at his or her résumé is a great skill. It's all too easy to throw a super person's bad résumé in the recycle bin, or spend a lot of time and effort interviewing someone who never should have been called in.

REVIEWING RÉSUMÉS

Let's use the definition of the most qualified people from the last chapter and apply it to the review of résumés.

- *Depth of experience (Expertise)*   How long has the candidate been working in this particular field, and how sophisticated or difficult were the projects he or she worked on? For example, does the person have two years of C++ development or ten years of C++ development? Did he or she write high-performance transaction code for a financial institution, or was he or she responsible only for building dialog box code for the institution's most recent application? Remember, past experience will expose a person's ability to master complex technology and apply it to the job. You're looking for people who have done sophisticated work in at least one focused area.

- *Happy feet (Commitment)*   One of the best ways to measure a candidate's commitment to a job is to check his or her résumé for job-hopping, or as it is sometimes called, "happy feet." If the person had four jobs in the last three years, you might want to question that person's long-term commitment. Although there could be legitimate reasons for the job changes, that behavior should be examined carefully.

- *Types of companies worked for in the past (Attitude, Team skills)*   Looking at the types of companies for which the candidate has worked in the past is also a good way to learn something about your potential employee. You want to find a person who will be a good match with the type of organization you have or are trying to create. Has the candidate always worked for large companies or for small companies? Has the candidate worked mostly in IS/IT groups or only at ISVs (independent software vendors)? Has the candidate spent most of his or her time working with government contracts, or have the last three jobs been with startup companies? Has the candidate worked primarily with commercial, shrink-wrapped software, or is the bulk of his or her experience with large, enterprise-wide projects?

The type of environment, the corporate culture, and the business segment a person has selected in the past can tell you a lot about the person without a face to face meeting. For example, if you're a startup company and a candidate has many startup companies on his or her résumé, that person might be a great fit. On the other hand, if you are interviewing a person who comes from a company that is heavy in processes and standards and you're trying to get a product to market quickly, you might want to pass on that particular candidate, especially if other factors are pointing in that direction as well.

◆ *Strong verbs and weak verbs (Behavior)*   The way a person writes about his or her prior experience can tell you a great deal. The best workers usually assume ownership of and responsibility for their tasks, and they are proud of them. Strong verbs usually are an indicator of this positive trait. Look for words like:

- Delivered
- Owned
- Managed
- Defined
- Wrote
- Integrated
- Drove
- Created

Weaker verbs generally imply less ownership and less responsibility. Using these verbs can signify that the candidate probably did not have complete ownership or authority. Look for words such as:

- Participated
- Reviewed
- Followed
- Helped
- Assisted
- Commented

- *Scope of responsibility (Behavior, Team skills)*   Review the scope of responsibility. How big was the project? How much was at stake? How important was it to the company? What would happen if the project failed? How many people were on the project?

- *Written skills (Team skills)*   Written communication is very important in software development. The cover letter and résumé will probably be the first examples of the applicant's writing skills you see. Unless you ask specifically for writing samples, they might be the only examples you will see. Do they read well? Are they too wordy? Are they too brief? Do you feel you understand what the person accomplished? Be sure to evaluate everything you receive from the candidate.

- *Breadth of experience (Thirst for knowledge)*   People's thirst for knowledge can be measured (to some extent) by looking at their range of work experience. In general, people who are driven to learn accept jobs and opportunities that allow them to try new things. A good measure of a person's breadth of experience can be found by noting whether he or she has demonstrated an ability to work at both high levels and low levels of abstraction. Does the person have the ability to work with the higher levels of the code (UI and logic, for example) as well as the internal levels of the technology (threads, memory management, OS internals, and the like)?

Not the Whole Story

Remember, the résumé doesn't tell the whole story. It doesn't even tell most of it. The résumé can only give you a hint about the person it describes and help you select a candidate to interview. Be sure to look for life experiences in the cover letter and in the résumé. They can sometimes show important traits that might apply to the job you have. Perhaps the ability to master multiple musical instruments shows the ability to work in multiple programming languages or environments, the ability to excel in an outdoor sport shows an adventurous nature, or military training shows discipline.

Phone Screening

You also might want to screen candidates on the phone before you schedule them for an interview. This process can be a very effective tool for getting some additional information about the candidate, and a great time-saver as well. It can help you clarify which position may be the best fit for the candidate or rule out the need to interview at all. The following are some guidelines for when to phone screen:

◆ *When you want to learn more about a candidate*   If you aren't sure about a candidate, sometimes a phone screening is the best way to help you decide whether or not he or she will fit your position. As I said earlier, the résumé is not the whole story, so when you're in doubt, get more information in a phone screening. Make sure to get the critical information you need to either pass on the candidate or bring him or her in for an interview.

Back at Work

When we wanted to have some fun at work, we would look at all the old résumés of the people we had hired years before. It was remarkable (and quite humorous) how bad their résumés were, compared to the talent they actually had or developed. I would occasionally block out a person's name and ask people on the team if they thought we should hire that person based on his or her résumé. The answers proved very interesting!

◆   *When you need to make contact but can't do it in person*   If schedule conflicts prevent you from setting up a timely interview, use a phone call to make first contact, establish a relationship, and confirm the position. For example, if you have a position that will develop the next generation of user interfaces for a market-leading PDA, make sure the candidate is aware of it. If you have a great team and a compelling place to work, you want the candidate to know this as well. These steps can help keep the candidate interested in your company while he or she explores other opportunities, and they help you decide if you want to increase your involvement with the individual.

INTERVIEWING CANDIDATES

You've finally got a good candidate coming in. The interview is next. Below are some important guidelines to help you effectively interview candidates for your open positions.

THE INTERVIEW TEAM

Everyone who will work closely with this person should be involved with the interviewing process. Remember, you're building a team, and it's critical that the other team members accept this person. It will be easier for them to do this if they have participated in the selection and want him or her to be part of the project.

KEY TOPICS

The key topics for the interview should be those attributes that I have previously discussed:

◆   Expertise

◆   Commitment

◆   Attitude

◆   Behavior

◆   Team skills

◆   Thirst for knowledge

EXPERTISE EVALUATION

An important interviewing technique is the evaluation of the person's area of expertise. It's a good idea to have the candidate meet with the functional lead or functional experts on your team. This might be your development lead, quality assurance lead, or technical writing lead. Make sure that your experts take the time to understand what the person has done and how well he or she did it.

Here's a simple tip: Even if you as the interviewer don't know as much about a subject as the candidate does, you can still ask many questions that probe the person's knowledge. Careful listening and good follow-up questions are key. For example:

- "What are threads?"

- "How do they work?"

- "Why would you want to use them?"

- "What are the common problems of threads?"

- "How would you describe the most complicated threading problem you had to solve?"

Frankly, you could ask this same set of questions about many technology topics, including COM controls, Sun servers, and Oracle databases. If the answers get shorter and shallower, you're probably digging below their comfort level. But if the candidate can easily speak volumes and provide real world illustrations, you've probably got a candidate who knows his or her stuff.

Back at Work

At NuMega, we were contacted by a candidate whose résumé indicated that he was an architect of a complicated COM-based system, so we asked our own COM experts to interview him. At the beginning of his interview, the candidate was asked to sketch out his design on a white board and then walk through the object models and design considerations. The interviewee drew a single box on the board, stared at it for quite a while, and then said, "Yep, you caught me, I lied on my résumé. I didn't design it." Lesson learned: Always make sure candidates can do what they say they can do.

KEY QUESTIONS

Your interview questions should be focused on the candidate's prior behavior, not just on hypothetical situations for which candidates usually know the "right" answer. You want to find out how he or she works under real conditions. Finding out how people behaved in past jobs is a good way to predict how they'll handle situations in their new job. Let's look at some general questions in the focus areas. These are by no means complete, but they can serve as examples of the kinds of open-ended, searching questions on key topics that you'd want to discuss.

- *Expertise*
  - Describe the last time you needed technical help with a problem. How long did you wait? How did you approach others? What was the result?

  - Tell me about a really difficult problem you had to debug. What was it? How did you find it? What was the fix?

  - Tell me about a new piece of code you had to pick up in a short amount of time. How did you do it? Were you successful? Why?

- *Commitment*
  - What was the most difficult part of your previous project? How did you feel about it? What was your role in it? What was the outcome?

  - Tell me about a time when your project had to respond to external changes. What happened? What was the team's response? What was your response?

Back at Work

One of our developer's favorite questions was, "Do you have a development-level system at home?" If the candidate didn't, our developer usually wasn't interested in the candidate. He was looking for people who were nuts about this stuff, who were happy to invest their own time and money on it, and who would most likely work at developing software for free if they couldn't get paid. He was looking for people who shared his passion.

◆ *Attitude*

  ◆ Describe the last time you missed a deadline. What happened? What was your response? What happened next?

  ◆ Can you describe the last time you were under a lot of pressure? What was your response? How did you handle it?

◆ *Behavior*

  ◆ Can you describe the last time you went out of your way to help someone else? Why did you do it? What was the result?

  ◆ Can you tell me the last time you put in extra effort even though no one asked you to and no one knew what you did?

◆ *Team skills*

  ◆ Describe the most difficult person you had to work with. What made him or her so difficult? What was your response? How did you feel?

  ◆ What are the most important principles for working well with others? Why? How have you exhibited these?

◆ *Thirst for knowledge*

  ◆ How do you stay educated? What books or magazines do you read, and which shows do you attend?

  ◆ Can you describe what is happening in the marketplace today for X? What's likely to happen in the future?

FEEDBACK AND CONCLUDING INTERVIEWS

Don't go it alone. Give your feedback to the rest of the interview team. Discuss the pros and cons of the candidate, and the areas that need further inquiry. (Don't try to bias each other; just discuss each of your areas of concern.)

There are times when it's pretty clear that the candidate is not a possibility for the open position. Either the candidate is not matching up to his or her résumé, or he or she is making comments that show he or she wouldn't be a fit for the team. Don't be afraid to end the interview if it's clear it's not going to work out. In general, we had a rule that if two people agreed that the interview was not worth continuing, they could end it without completing the rest of the interviewing schedule. There's no reason to waste your time or the candidate's.

CANDIDATE TESTING

Testing the candidate's ability can be very revealing. It's often an important pre-employment step used by startups and small companies to find out more about a candidate than an interview will indicate. To be effective, the test must not require a great deal of external or supporting information. On the other hand, it needs to be complicated enough to see how the candidate works through tough problems.

Often the most important part of the test is not the test itself but how the person reacts to it. Did the candidate panic? Did he or she just give up after five minutes? Did he or she find a creative or unique solution? Did he or she put in the effort? Did the candidate make good progress even if he or she couldn't finish or get the answer?

People often feel that interviews are stressful enough without testing. That might be true, but working in a software development environment can be a lot more stressful than that. You need to make sure you have people who can handle some level of stress.

Back at Work

For years, we gave the same programming test to every developer. It was a straightforward test that required no setup or external knowledge from manuals. The candidates were asked to write a program that could print its source code to the screen exactly, without performing any file input. Although it was a difficult test for most candidates, it revealed a lot about them. Some people gave up in minutes, while others would send back the answer later because they couldn't solve it during the interview. One person even called the solution in during his flight home! Isn't that the kind of person you want on your team?

WORK SAMPLES

Another means of testing candidates' skill is to ask for a sample of their work. Many UI developers, tech writers, human factors engineers, and developers can easily provide these samples for you. For example, UI developers and human factors engineers can show screen shots of their shipping products, while tech writers can present the documentation or help files they have worked on. QA engineers often have old test plans or other supporting documentation. By carefully looking at their prior work you can gain a good insight into their prior experience and skill set. When you can go either way with a candidate, a sample can really push you in the right direction.

THE SELL

If all is going well in the interview process, you'll start to see the candidate as a strong contender for the position. At this point you need to be able to articulate why this position, this company, and this work environment would make a great match for him or her. Good candidates have many opportunities, so it's critical that you be able to succinctly describe the advantages of working for you.

To develop a strong sell message, ask the following questions about your own project, group, or company:

- What technology opportunities are available?
- What type of products will the candidate be working on?
- What type of company will the candidate be working for?
- What are the unique work opportunities?
- What are the unique work environment advantages?

Note that salary and benefits aren't part of the sell message. Those are part of the compensation package, which I'll talk about shortly. You don't want to hire someone who wants the job based only on the compensation package that comes with it. You should know the candidate is interested in the job before getting into details about the numbers.

Back at Work

At NuMega our sell line was crystal clear and everyone knew it by heart. For most people, it worked like magic:

- Q: What technology opportunities are available?
- A: Low-level Windows internals.

- Q: What type of products will the candidate be working on?
- A: Developer tools, debugging products.

- Q: What type of company will the candidate be working for?
- A: A rapidly growing commercial software vendor.

- Q: What are the unique work opportunities?
- A: Using advanced, unannounced technologies from Microsoft and Intel; working with an elite development team.

- Q: What are the unique work environment advantages?
- A: A casual developer-oriented environment that mixes business with pleasure.

THE DECISION

When it's time to make a decision, be sure to get everyone's input. Gather everyone together in a room to discuss their thoughts and observations. When you do this, you will discover one of three things:

- You have a winner.
- You don't have a winner.
- It's not clear what you have at all—you have different opinions.

Only make an offer if it's clear that you have a winner—don't take unnecessary chances. If, after much discussion and thought, there's serious reservation from any team member, it's usually best not to go forward. It's important to respect each team member's opinion. It's particularly important for management not to force a candidate on the team. It's also far more likely that a team will accept and help a new team member if they have been part of the interviewing and selection process.

THE CLOSER

When you are finished with the interviewing process and are certain that you want to hire the candidate, you might need to use a closer. Sometimes a candidate will be pondering multiple offers or have some doubts or issues that can't be addressed by the recruiters alone. A closer is someone who can put to rest any remaining issues or hesitancy in the candidate's mind and is skilled at closing the deal. This may involve phone calls at home, an early morning breakfast, a late evening dinner, and some delicate negotiations. But just the fact that you are giving special attention tends to show the candidate that he or she is valued and important to the organization and can greatly increase your chance of landing the candidate.

THE OFFER

When it's time to make an offer, it should be done quickly and with a solid initial offer. You want to demonstrate to the candidate that he or she will be an important part of your team. Remember, you're only hiring the best. There's no need to fool around.

I strongly suggest a package that includes a solid base salary and performance incentives. This typically takes the form of a performance bonus and stock options that are appropriate for the level of contribution expected from the new employee.

FOLLOW-UP

Be prepared to follow up with candidates who don't accept immediately. Again, talented people have many opportunities. Don't let the offer just sit there. You need to follow up with e-mails, letters, or phone calls within a few days of the offer. Don't lose contact with the candidate at this critical stage. If there are other issues, offers, or complications, you need to know about them. If you don't hear back in a few days after the offer has been extended, be sure to follow up.

WHAT TO DO WHEN YOU LOSE A CANDIDATE

The decision making process can get emotional, and small things can often make the difference. When a candidate says no, make sure it's for a solid reason and not because of something that can be easily resolved. This requires you to really understand why a person declined an offer. You shouldn't just take a "better offer" answer at face value. Make sure you understand the reasons behind the answer.

Back at Work

We once had a good QA candidate who refused our offer because of a "personal commitment" to his family. As we poked at this some more, and after some discussion, we found out it was a promise to take his family to Disney World. He thought he couldn't get the time off due to our time critical release. His impression was essentially correct—we really needed people to come on board and help get the product out the door. But when we learned what his reservation was, we discussed it with the leads and agreed that he was a valuable enough addition to the team to merit accommodating his schedule so he could keep his commitment to his family.

On another occasion, though, we made an offer to a great developer who then decided that he needed to stay with his current project because they needed him and he felt compelled to stick it out. We were sorry to hear this of course, but we respected his position and hoped he'd call back when the project was over. We didn't try to talk him out of his commitment. You should never try to talk someone out of the very same values that you are recruiting for. Eventually, he did call back and we hired him on the spot. We were willing to wait to get him and could be confident he'd treat us with the same commitment he'd shown to his previous employer.

RETAINING EMPLOYEES

Now that you're getting top-quality people, it's important that you retain them. There are three main reasons why people stay with their current employers:

◆ *Professional* Good people like to work hard. They take great pride in what they are doing and want to know that it's going to mean something. People must know that their work matters and is appreciated. They need to know that they are making a difference to the company and are a part of its success. Be sure to take the time to recognize these needs and provide feedback on both a personal level and on a group level.

On the other hand, even if you've got the most important project on the planet, you must make sure people stay fresh and work on new things over time. New challenges, new people, and new technology—it's important to move people to new assignments or even to new products to keep things interesting and exciting.

◆ *Financial* Industry studies say that compensation is not the most important reason why people change jobs. Although this might be true, if you've got a staff of superstars, you need to compensate them very well. The overall compensation package should include a base salary, bonuses for special accomplishments, and long-term options for sharing in the company's success. Compensating people in this manner is important because it gives people an incentive to go the extra mile and can lock them in financially if the stock price rises over time.

People who are this talented rarely have a problem finding a higher-paying job. But if you have a better than average compensation package, people will feel they are being treated well, and higher compensation packages offered elsewhere will have less appeal. The risk of losing a person because of money is even less likely if you value the employee in the other ways mentioned as well. And, if a person is solely after the money, he or she probably isn't a good fit for the team anyway.

◆ *Social* A workplace that is also a great social environment can do wonders for retaining employees. If people have social relationships with their co-workers and enjoy the working environment, they are far less likely to risk a job change (as long as their professional and financial needs are met). Don't underestimate the power of a couple of PCs for each team member and a nice office. Mix these in with a healthy and active social environment and you've got a recipe for keeping the team together.

TECHNIQUES FOR RETENTION

The best way to keep employees is to address the three areas above as equally as possible. Although excellence might be easier to achieve in one area than another, the real benefit to the company occurs when you have a good balance among the three. Here are some pointers for achieving this balance.

◆ *Professional*

  ◈ Make sure people are developing new skills and trying new things.

  ◈ Make sure people know that they are both responsible and accountable for their work.

  ◈ Make sure people know the importance of their products or projects.

  ◈ Acknowledge excellent work privately and publicly.

  ◈ Move people between teams frequently to encourage growth and sharing.

  ◈ Know the team members' career goals, and make sure opportunities for advancement are there for them.

◆ *Financial*

  ◈ Make sure salaries and compensation are above market standard for the most talented employees.

  ◈ Give bonuses for excellent accomplishments.

  ◈ Award stock options to key employees.

◆ *Social*

  ◈ Assign a buddy to all new employees to guide them though the first few weeks.

  ◈ Provide extracurricular activities (volleyball games, trips to the movies).

  ◈ Nurture social relationships with team building activities to break down barriers.

  ◈ Encourage social activities both at work and away from the workplace—don't rely on the annual holiday party!

COMMON PROBLEMS AND SOLUTIONS

The following are some of the typical problems and questions that surface when applying these techniques, and some solutions to those problems.

INTERVIEWING PROBLEMS AND SOLUTIONS

◆ *Poor interviewing processes or techniques*   Poor interviewing processes and techniques are a very common problem. Most interviewers are either new to interviewing or not very good at it. Make sure the people who will be interviewing candidates are educated and trained, even informally, on what they are expected to do and how to do it. If a team member continually evaluates candidates just on intuition and can only give a shoulder shrug when asked for justifications, you may end up hiring the wrong people or passing over great candidates.

◆ *A poorly defined position*   Unless this is an exploratory interview, you should be interviewing for a specific position. If you don't know what the roles and responsibilities are for the position, you will get very different opinions from the members of the interview team about the candidate's qualifications. Be sure to have a clearly written job description for each position that is available to all interviewers well before the candidate arrives.

◆ *Spending too much time with an unqualified candidate*   Don't spend any longer than you need with a candidate. It's OK to let the candidate know that there's not a match. Make sure you have a well-understood process for dismissing a candidate before the end of the interview. There's no need to waste the candidate's time or your time on an interview that's not going well.

◆ *Too much or too little selling*   Some organizations don't sell themselves enough. The candidate is interviewed so closely that there is no room left for him or her to explore the position. The candidate is left with too many questions and doesn't know if this position is right for him or her. Other organizations sell too much and don't actually interview the candidate. You need to know your company's selling points and deliver them at the appropriate time, but this should not get in the way of the interview process.

◆ *No closer* Make sure you have one or more people who really know how to close a candidate. You don't want to let good candidates walk out the door with significant questions or an incomplete understanding of the opportunity. If the candidate has not accepted the offer, you want to make sure you have a senior person who can address his or her issues or questions. This person needs to be able to speak to a wide range of issues, including the company vision or future, the individual's career growth and opportunities, and the ability to compare and contrast alternative offers.

◆ *Moving slowly* Great candidates are hard to find. When you're sure you've found one, you must move quickly. Nights and weekends are fair game. Don't hesitate to meet a candidate for an interview at night, or fly him or her in for a weekend interview with the team. Be prepared for same-day interviews and offers. I'm not suggesting you rush the interview process when there's no need, but there are often circumstances that will require you to make decisions quickly and outside normal working hours.

As a result, make sure you have the internal process set up to get an offer out immediately. Time is of the essence when recruiting great talent, and you'll be competing against other companies most of the time. There's nothing more frustrating than finding a great candidate and then hearing he or she accepted another offer before yours arrived.

RETENTION PROBLEMS AND SOLUTIONS

◆ *Improper balance* The most common retention problems can be described in terms of an improper balance among the professional, financial, and social factors. You can't successfully sacrifice one for another over a long period of time. Be sure to evaluate your team or company's balance among professional satisfaction, financial compensation, and social support on a regular basis. Don't wait for problems to occur before you take action.

◆ *Turnover* Some level of turnover must be expected. Personal situations and priorities change. People leave for reasons that you can't control—a new baby, a shorter commute, or a need to be near relatives. On the other hand, turnover can be a sign of serious problems in the team or the organization. To help make the reasons for turnover clear over time, be sure to interview individuals before they leave the company and have an open mind regarding their comments. If there are internal problems, be sure to ask others on the team if they share these concerns. In larger organizations, it's also a good idea to keep a running list of the reasons people have left. This information could help make trends clear and provide justification for changes.

3

Project Organization

No matter how talented your people are, they still need the right organizational structure to do their best work. Projects suffer from a lack of organization and unclear roles and responsibilities. Each person needs to understand his or her role and how it fits into the larger project context.

In this chapter, I detail the organizational structure used at NuMega. I also address the roles, responsibilities, and skill sets the team members needed to execute this model.

NuMega's Organizational Structure

Teams, not individuals, build software. A development team is a group of people with different engineering skills who work together on a common project. Because of the complexity involved in software development, you want a group of people with the diverse sets of skills and abilities necessary to deliver a product. The following is a list of the disciplines you will need on the team:

- ◆ *Core team*   Disciplines that are 100 percent involved in the production of a new software product
    - ◆ Project management
    - ◆ Software development
    - ◆ Quality assurance
    - ◆ User education
    - ◆ Human factors engineering
    - ◆ Release engineering

- ◆ *Supporting team*   Disciplines that have other priorities beyond the software's development but have an important role to play in the project
    - ◆ Product management and marketing
    - ◆ Software support
    - ◆ Beta administration

It's very important that these functional groups are part of the project effort from the very beginning. The more people can participate, understand, review, and critique the definition of the product, the better they can prepare and execute their own plans and feel part of the project's success.

In addition, to deliver your project as soon as possible, you need all these teams working in parallel throughout the entire development cycle. In Chapter 11 you'll learn how you can build mutual time-coordinated milestones into your project schedule to support this goal.

If, on the other hand, the staffing on your project is missing entire functional groups or is severely understaffed in one or more areas, you are not going to have the deep understanding, synergy, and incremental progress that is so important to software development. I'm not suggesting every staff member must be present on day one, but it's important that you have representatives—hopefully these are the leads from each of the functional groups—participating from the first day. Don't underestimate the importance of this statement or the difficulty of achieving it.

MANAGEMENT

As an example of how the management structure of a small company can function with optimum efficiency, let me detail how NuMega management handled the challenges we faced. Like most startup companies (and most development groups), we were short on resources and had a lot of work to do in a small amount of time. We knew we had to have an efficient organizational structure that would take advantage of the talented people we worked so hard to attract. We needed to have a structure that would respond quickly to challenges, keep the overhead at a minimum, and support growth. To meet these requirements we used a flat organizational structure in which a single project manager was in charge of the overall product development. This person's responsibilities included overseeing all the software developers, quality assurance engineers, release engineers, and technical writers—all the people who are part of the core team. This is a crucial point: All the talent was brought together under the direction of one manager who would oversee the project. (Over the years we had both male and female project managers; in this discussion I'll alternate between "he" and "she" to refer to these managers.)

The other people (technical support, beta administration, product management, and marketing) did not report to the project manager; they did, however, work directly with the project manager to make sure their needs and issues were addressed. This worked well because the priorities of those other functions were focused on tasks (market analysis, pricing, call handling, ads, and so on) that did not involve the day-to-day development of the product. However, because everyone had a single project manager, communications with those other functional teams were clearer and simpler.

Although this organizational structure worked well, we increased its effectiveness by using the following principles:

◆ *Flexible resource utilization*   The project manager was able to allocate and direct the team's resources for any single problem, issue, or initiative. This arrangement allowed the project manager to align resources with the immediate internal priorities of the project and allowed the resources to be fully utilized and quickly balanced with the rapidly changing needs of the project.

◆ *Ownership of dedicated resources*   The project manager owned all the resources while the project was ongoing. The entire team worked on the project full time from the day the project started until the day it shipped. There was a single set of people working with the same set of priorities, toward the same goal, with one person in charge of it all. With this structure, we were able to get everyone participating and contributing to the product early on, and each felt a greater sense of ownership and commitment as a result. People also had a better understanding of the product features and constraints, as well as why and how certain decisions were made. This involvement translated into better plans, better schedules, better testing, and better documentation.

Back at Work

At NuMega, the most important project meeting was usually the kick-off meeting. We put people in a room and told them that the only way this product would get done was if the people in the room did it. Each person had to be dedicated to the project until it shipped, and each person had to have a specific role and responsibility. If the project was successful or well-received, it would be because of what the team did together. And if it failed, it would also be because of the people in that room. This level of direct accountability, supported by the team's ability to make many of its own decisions, produced terrific results.

◆ *Centralized decision making*   Because a single project manager oversaw the entire project, he had the ability to quickly break deadlocks and make critical decisions when consensus building failed.

◆ *Clearer lines of communication*   A single project manager provided a focal point for everyone in the company who had concerns and issues that needed to be discussed. Communication channels were clear and simple, allowing issues to be handled with greater efficiency and effectiveness—not just with the core team but with the support teams as well.

◆ *Entrepreneurial responsibility*   The project manager did not just manage the project—he was expected to be one of the product's entrepreneurs. He had to know the competition and the direction of the marketplace, and really understand the value of the features we were adding to the release. Without this information, he would not have been able to evaluate the implementation as it emerged and assure that the work was hitting the mark. The project manager was partnered with the product manager, the person who articulates the market requirements and maintains the business case for the product. Both the product manager and the project manager contributed to all areas—specifically, licensing, pricing, promotion, and marketing. Together, these two people were responsible for the ultimate success of the product. They had both the responsibility and the authority to make key decisions. Because they had this much control, they were able to make those decisions quickly and effectively. The team, knowing they were working directly with the decision-makers, knew their ideas and their performance were both visible and crucial to the success of the project.

LEADS

We also assigned leads to each of the functional areas. The leads provided expert leadership in their respective disciplines and worked very closely with the project manager and other leads throughout the project. Leads played a critical leadership role on the team by driving issues and making decisions in the key areas that were assigned to them. This arrangement allowed us to add more people in a functional area very easily because we had someone who drove that portion of the product. Figure 3-1 shows the relationship between the project manager and the leads of the functional areas.

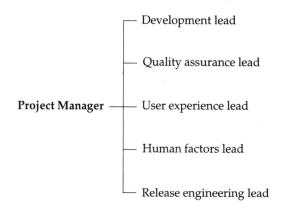

Development lead

Quality assurance lead

Project Manager —— User experience lead

Human factors lead

Release engineering lead

FIGURE 3-1   *Relationships between project manager and functional leads*

Because the people we hired were highly qualified and experienced, they needed little management supervision. They needed only to be told what the plan was and what they were responsible for. This tended to keep the teams smaller and more cohesive, which increased our ability to respond to changes. But most importantly, it allowed us to keep the essential resources of the project under the control of a single manager who would be very close to the day-to-day operations of the team.

ROLES AND RESPONSIBILITIES

Let's take a look at the basic roles and responsibilities for each of the functions that contribute to product development.

PROJECT MANAGER

Clearly, the project manager plays an essential role in the project. The following is a list of the numerous roles and responsibilities that the project manager needs to perform:

◆   *Staffing and personnel management*   The project manager is responsible for building and managing the team. She also oversees staffing, career planning, retention, reviews, and morale. She has to hire new team members, grow people's skills and talents, and keep individuals motivated and content over the course of the development effort.

◆ *Defining and executing the project plan*   The project manager drives the definition and execution of the project plan. She assembles the teams who are submitting requirements and drives consensus and closure. When the requirements are complete, she builds a project plan that addresses the development, quality assurance, user education, release engineering, and human factors initiatives required to build the product. The plan also addresses the other key parts of the product, such as schedule, implementation technology, staffing, assumptions, and risks. This doesn't necessarily mean she owns all the decisions, but she is responsible for driving the project deliverables to closure with all the stakeholders and clearly communicating the overall plan to the project team. All these issues will be discussed in greater detail in Part II.

Throughout the development process, a wide variety of feature tradeoffs will need to be made. It is the project manager's responsibility to make sure these decisions are made in a timely and effective manner and are supported by and communicated to the team. If these changes result in a change in the product scope, however, then the decision and its ramifications must be communicated to everyone involved.

Because the project manager is in charge of implementation of the feature set for the product as well as staffing and balancing resources, the project manager also oversees the schedule for the entire project. It's the project manager's responsibility to make sure the product stays on schedule and to take corrective action when problems occur.

The project manager creates a master schedule based on input from the team members for all activities on the project. This schedule is typically divided into milestones and base level deliverables. The project manager must continually review the product's schedule, make necessary changes, and communicate changes to the product development team, peer organizations (product management, technical support, and beta administration), and senior management. Scheduling will be covered in detail in Chapter 11.

◆ *Leading the team* The project manager is responsible for executing a smooth and efficient product development process. The project manager is the "lead blocker" for the team—clearing obstacles and securing whatever is necessary for the team to succeed. He must quickly identify problem areas, work toward speedy resolutions, and keep the project team focused and in harmony. He must also assume the role of coach and mentor, with enough knowledge and experience in the various disciplines to assess the team's progress and contribute when necessary.

◆ *Linking the teams* The project manager is the key communication link between the product development team and the product management and marketing team. The project manager is responsible for collecting input from these groups and working those needs into the project plan. He is also responsible for communicating issues or changes in the project plan to the product manager and marketing manager throughout the life of the project. The project manager should also review the product management and marketing plan and provide appropriate feedback.

The project manager also has to be the key communication link between the product development team, the technical support team, and the beta administration group. The project manager must address any critical issues that arise with the product while it is being tested at customer sites (the beta test) and after it has been released to customers.

◆ *Ensuring product readiness* The project manager is responsible for delivering the most complete and highest-quality product possible. As a result, the project manager has ultimate responsibility in the engineering organization for making sure that all the software, documentation, and human factors goals have been met.

DEVELOPMENT ENGINEERING

Engineering can be divided into three principal functions: development (or dev) lead, feature (or technical) lead, and software engineer. Figure 3-2 illustrates the relationships between these function groups.

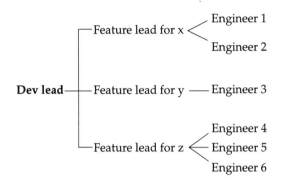

FIGURE 3-2   *Relationships among dev lead, feature lead, and engineers*

Dev Lead

The dev lead is the primary driver for the software development effort. There is usually only one person in this position. He or she plays a critical role in the engineering effort because this person must have enough experience and maturity to work through the many complex technical and personnel issues that occur during the course of the development cycle. These responsibilities include:

◆   Keeping the architecture and technical definition of the product on course

◆   Selecting key technology tools and standards

◆   Identifying and resolving all technical issues

◆   Acting as the technical mentor and sounding board for project members

◆   Overseeing and reviewing the user education, QA, and release engineering staff

- Monitoring the health (bug list) of the product
- Selecting and supervising of development tools, metrics, and standards
- And, of course—code, code, and code

Feature (or Technical) Leads

Feature leads are in charge of the development of a particular feature of the product, often based on or localized around a particular technology. Features tend to be broadly defined, such as "Integration with the IDE" or "Delivery of the database access API." Feature leads are responsible for:

- Coordinating architectural issues with other feature leads
- Contributing to and reviewing feature requirements
- Designing the feature
- Providing technical resources on the feature to QA and documentation staff
- And, of course—code, code, and code

Individual Software Engineers

Individual software engineers are assigned to a feature, usually under the direction of a single feature lead. They are responsible for implementing specific aspects of the feature, such as "Integrating the X, Y and Z windows into the IDE." Or "Writing the create, update and delete methods of the database services API." Their responsibilities include:

- Implementing the feature
- Testing the feature
- Fixing bugs in the feature
- Supporting the user education team's documentation of the feature
- Supporting the QA team's testing of the feature

QUALITY ASSURANCE (QA)

The quality assurance (QA) team members are responsible for defining and executing the test plan for the project. To make sure that there is a true partnership between the people who write the code and the people who test the code, the QA team has roles and responsibilities that parallel those of the development team.

Traditionally, QA teams are separated from the development team so they can act as an independent authority on the quality of the software; otherwise, a "fox guarding the chicken coop" scenario is likely to develop. On the other hand, having a QA group with their own manager who is a peer to the project manager can create a "them vs. us" environment. Over time the groups can drift apart and create an adversarial relationship that can poison everything you're trying to do.

At NuMega, we avoided both of these problems by putting the final quality decisions in the hands of the project manager. He was required to deliver a quality product and would be held accountable for any problems with it. He had to rely on the QA team to verify that the product was ready to ship. With this structure (Figure 3-3), the QA team could still be independent because they had their own lead and sub-team. However, because they reported to the same project manager as the developers, they still felt, were treated, and acted as part of the same team. Quality assurance is covered in more detail in Chapter 6.

Project Manager
(Owns timely delivery of a quality product)

Dev lead
(Owns implementation)

QA lead
(Owns quality assurance)

FIGURE 3-3   *QA and development relationship*

QA Lead

The QA lead is responsible for defining and executing a quality assurance process throughout the development cycle. The QA lead has to have strong personal QA skills and the ability to direct and lead the rest of the QA team. This person is responsible for these areas:

- ◆ *Defining and maintaining the product's test plan*   The test plan describes the testing effort for the project: what will be tested, how it will be tested, and when it will be tested. Additional needs, resources, and issues are also addressed.

- ◆ *Executing the test plan*   The QA lead is responsible for the execution of the test plan throughout the development cycle. The QA lead matches the testing of the product with the specific base levels and milestones of the product's development schedule and ensures that testing of the new features occurs in a timely manner.

- ◆ *Automating test beds*   To reduce testing time, the QA lead is responsible for driving the automation of the most critical tests, as identified in the test plan. The test bed is created and maintained by the test team, but the overall responsibility for the test bed belongs to the QA lead.

- ◆ *Performing regression tests*   The QA lead is responsible for making sure the regression tests are run after every build of the system. These tests (also known as smoke tests) are preferably done at night so the results will be ready in the morning. The QA lead is responsible for reviewing the results on a daily basis and logging new bugs into the bug tracking system.

- ◆ *Testing tools, metrics, and standards*   The QA lead is responsible for selecting and maintaining the quality assurance tools, metrics, and standards during the product's development—just like the dev lead does for the development team. For example, the QA lead is responsible for the integrity of the data in the bug tracking systems—just like the dev lead is responsible for the integrity of the data in the source code management system.

Automation Engineer

The automation engineer is focused on creating automated test beds, as defined in the test plan. This person is typically highly skilled in test automation tools, scripting, and often programming as well. Automation engineers are assigned the automation of a set of features and focus on testing specific, quantifiable parts of the product, which allows them to work closely with the engineers who own the development of those features. The automation engineer has a narrower set of responsibilities than the other team members because of the need to have automation ready once the features have been coded. His or her responsibilities include:

◆   Test bed planning

◆   Test bed automation

◆   Tools evaluation and assessment

QA Specialist

The QA specialist is responsible for the execution of the test plan as defined by the QA lead. The QA specialist typically plays the "user" of the product and knows the set of features (if not the whole product) extremely well. He or she should be especially adept at ad-hoc and user interface (UI) "fit and finish" testing. This person's basic responsibilities include:

◆   Testing installation, UI, and features, as directed by the test plan

◆   Executing automated test beds

◆   Analyzing and logging automated test bed results or problems

◆   Closing bug reports

◆   Setting up testing environments

USER EDUCATION

The user education team provides educational material for the user. This typically involves hard copy documentation, online help, tutorials, and quick reference cards.

User Education Lead

The user education lead is responsible for creating the product's overall documentation plan. She uses her knowledge of the product and the needs of the customer to present a plan that shows what documentation will be written or updated and when this work will be completed, taking into account the available resources.

The user education lead is also responsible for defining the documentation standards (or contributing to them) and making sure the product stays current with emerging writing conventions and technology.

User Education Specialist

In addition to writing and producing the documentation, a secondary set of responsibilities for the user education team involves usability and quality. Often a user education specialist can find glaring holes in these areas because she works with the product from the user's point of view. Let me provide two examples of how this works:

- Because the user education specialist writes the documentation describing how the product should be used, she is often the first to uncover inconsistencies and usage problems in the product's feature set or implementation. It's quite common for the user education specialist to say, "Gee, I know I was in the meeting when we reviewed the specifications, but now that I'm writing the user's manual, it's clear that the user needs to perform ten steps to complete this task, and that just doesn't make sense." In this way the user education specialist is performing a very valuable usability double-check early in the development cycle and is providing corrective feedback.

- The user education specialist should be using the software on almost a daily basis to accurately document newly implemented features and to stay abreast of changes. This regular use of the product often uncovers all sorts of quality problems early in the development cycle, when they can more easily be solved. Although the idea is not for the user education team do a first pass QA check, because they are trying to use the different pieces of the software together, they can uncover a number of important bugs that might not have been identified until much later. In this respect, the user education specialist performs another check on the quality of the product and can often give a very realistic opinion of the quality of the software.

HUMAN FACTORS ENGINEERING

How the user experiences the product is crucial to whether or not your software will succeed in the market. The software interface, documentation, and packaging must all work together to create a positive image for the customer.

At NuMega, we also felt very strongly that the first 20 minutes with our product were crucial to its adoption and continued use. This is called the "Out of the Box" experience. If the user did not have a positive experience, and if we did not solve specific problems quickly and easily, it was unlikely the product would be used regularly or be truly valued by the customer.

To address these needs, we employed human factors engineers. The human factors lead for our projects had overall responsibility for translating product requirements into the fundamental tasks that the user has to perform. He then translated these tasks into a model of the user interface. We found these deliverables were essential to organizing, optimizing, and prioritizing the rest of the team's work. For example, the QA team would focus on creating tests for the key tasks identified by the human factors team first, while the documentation team would make sure that these tasks received the most attention in the tutorials and user's guide. We wanted to make sure that these tasks—the key valuable proposition of the product—would not be done late or have too little time devoted to them.

This point is crucial. The entire team must know which tasks are the most important to the user and how these tasks are implemented in the software. If someone on the team doesn't know this, the team can end up working at cross-purposes during the development cycle. Have you ever seen a developer or QA person spending too much time developing or testing a seemingly obscure feature when some of the main features are not working well or not working at all? Have you ever seen a team argue and bicker endlessly about the UI late in a beta cycle? Chances are that they have a different understanding of the priorities of the user and have never agreed up front on how these tasks are going to be supported. The fundamentals of human factors engineering are covered in Chapter 10.

The human factors engineer must have the ability to perform the following tasks:

◆ Translating requirements into key tasks

◆ Creating a user interface design (windows, dialogs, layouts, and so on) for these tasks

◆ Testing the design and securing approval from the team

◆ Defining a successful "out of box" experience

◆ Performing "fit and finish" reviews of the user interface

◆ Following up with customers after the release

RELEASE ENGINEERING

The release engineer provides the basic services that are needed to keep your development model operational. It is essential work that must be performed either by dedicated resources or by your developers. If necessary, extend the schedule to accommodate the work. Don't be fooled into thinking you can do without this function. You can't—not if you want to release software on time. I'll discuss release engineering in more detail in Chapter 7.

In general, release engineering has three major functions:

◆ *Building and maintaining an appropriate build environment for the product*   The build of the project is an essential first step and needs to be completed as early as possible. Building the product every day is key to your project's success and is required to implement many of the concepts in this book.

◆ *Building and maintaining the installation procedure*   The frequent building of the software reaches its full value when it can be automatically installed. You will also need to maintain and update the installation procedure over the course of the development cycle and be sure to keep resources assigned to this task.

◆ *Maintaining and administrating the source code management systems*   It's important to have a single person own the maintenance and administration of the source code management system. Source code management tools will be covered in the next chapter.

PRODUCT MANAGEMENT AND MARKETING

From the engineering team's point of view, the product management and marketing team has two roles. The first involves "input," and the second involves "output."

From the input side, the product management and marketing team defines the market segments, business requirements, and product requirements for the product. It's essential to the ultimate success of the development effort to have clear, concise, and practical business requirements and justifications. In addition to product feature input, bundling, installation, licensing, and documentation requirements should be included as well.

From the output side, the engineering team relies on the product management and marketing team to present the product externally. This effort includes advertising, sales training, sales collateral, analyst briefings, press releases and briefings, and Web updates.

The engineering team is dependent on the product management and marketing team to communicate the results of their work, to launch the product, and to make sure it is successful in the marketplace. The engineering effort will be for naught if the marketing effort fails to get the software noticed. The cooperation and team spirit between these two functions is critically important. The more these two teams work together, share ideas, and feel like one effort, the greater the likelihood that corrections will be made quickly and effectively and the higher the chances of success.

You're not done when the product ships, though. You're done when the product hits its revenue, profit, or business goals. Ultimate success is not defined by shipping, but by winning in the market.

TECHNICAL SUPPORT

The technical support engineer will probably have the most regular customer contact after the product ships. He will be representing the development team to the customer every day. This individual plays a very important and valuable role not just for customers, but also for the development team. Specifically, the development team counts on the technical support team to accomplish the tasks listed on the next page.

- Providing feature requirements to make the product easier to support

- Raising important quality or feature issues to the development team during the beta cycle and after the product ships

- Providing call-handling statistics (type, severity, and volume) to support and demonstrate the need for fixes or changes

- Assisting the development of the project by acting as an objective third party on UI issues, by checking out early (alpha) releases of the product, by helping with QA crunches, and by assisting in bug fixes if the team falls behind

To support these activities, you should designate an individual as the support lead for the product effort. The support lead should have a close professional relationship with the project manager and all the leads on the project. He or she will be part of the production effort from the beginning of the development cycle to the end.

During development, the support lead will have access to the source files, internal documentation, plans, and schedules. After the software has shipped, he or she will work on urgent issues with the leads and provide regular reports on the success of the product in the field, backed up with critical data that shows the good, the bad, and the ugly.

Don't underestimate the importance of the technical support team. They are part of the engineering group and need to be properly integrated into the engineering effort. Great technical support can overcome all sorts of product deficiencies in the field and turn an unhappy customer into a much happier one.

BETA PROGRAM ADMINISTRATOR

The beta administrator is responsible for planning, managing, and executing a beta program. A well-run beta program can significantly enhance the success of the product by giving you real-world feedback. In fact, beta programs are so important that I've dedicated a whole chapter to them. But for now, simply consider the fundamental responsibilities of a beta program administrator:

- Recruiting, qualifying, and signing up beta site candidates

- Distributing beta instructions and software

◆ Sending surveys and other follow-up material to candidates

◆ Publishing beta testing results internally

◆ Refining the beta testing process over time

COMMON PROBLEMS AND SOLUTIONS

The following are some of the typical problems and questions that surface when applying these techniques, and some solutions to those problems:

◆ *Lack of definition or too much definition*   Even the most talented people need some definition of their roles and responsibilities. They need to have the basics in place so they know where to spend their time. These definitions should be detailed and task-oriented. However, don't get carried away or they might become too legalistic and rigid. You don't want your team quoting chapter and verse from the job description when you need to get the product out the door. You're trying to avoid major holes in execution, not micro-manage behavior. Use the job outlines presented in this chapter as examples.

◆ *Lack of balance*   Just because you have a model that encourages a balance of skill sets and functional expertise doesn't mean your project is actually being staffed that way. Be sure to check the balance of resources within your functional teams regularly. For example, does your team have the right number of QA people? It doesn't make sense to have 100 developers and only 4 or 5 QA people, even if those QA people have all the skills you need. The developer to QA ratio is critical in a project and needs to be balanced. Your ratio will depend on the needs of your project, but most organizations like to maintain a developer to QA ratio of between 2:1 and 4:1 . If you can't maintain this ratio, you will still need to perform the quality assurance work—it'll just take longer.

◆ *Lack of scalability*   One of the issues with the project model presented in this chapter is its scalability. As you add more people on a project—say, going from 20 to 100 individuals—you can't function with only one project manager. There are just too many people to manage. Fortunately, there are two ways to solve this problem.

First, there's the traditional solution, which is to add functional managers for each of the functional teams—development managers, quality assurance managers, technical writing managers, and so on. These managers assume many of the responsibilities of the project manager for their own disciplines. This solution works well in most cases, especially if the project remains homogenous—all 100 people working on the same product. With qualified managers, this model can work well and grow very large.

The second way is to create multiple small to mid-sized teams based on the organizational structure presented in this chapter. This plan works especially well if you have independent deliverables; for example, two products, two editions, or two independent pieces of the same product. You could assign a small number of people to these deliverables and keep the smaller project model that I've discussed here. While forming more teams eliminates the scalability problem, it can also create new problems of its own. For example, you now have a 100-person organization composed of 6 or 7 independently operating teams that are not leveraging the tools, standards, capital, processes, and information between the teams.

One of the best ways to handle this challenge is to appoint a strong functional expert (one each for development, QA, release engineering, user education, human factors) to lead the identification and resolution of common problems. These shared issues could involve common testing tools, establishment of a common testing lab, and definition of documentation standards, usability standards, and the like. The functional expert works with all the teams involved to solve their common problems and establish policies that increase the productivity of all. In some ways it's similar to the concept of a guild. For example, if all of the bankers in a particular town wanted to improve local commerce, they could form a banker's guild to discuss how to promote and improve banking-related issues. The same concept can work for quality assurance, documentation, release engineering, and so on. As long as you have leaders with strong functional expertise and leadership qualities, you can get this model to work.

4

Ranking and Culture

A lthough it is true that everyone is important and everyone contrib- utes, ranking is the arrangement of team members by contribution and significance to the organization. In discussing ranking, we explore the importance of individuals based on their contribution rather than on function or seniority.

This chapter also covers the culture of software development companies. Your company's culture can affect your group's productivity and ability to ship on time as much as any other factor.

RANKING

Ranking is not a new concept. One example of it is how some sports organizations designate their most important performers as "franchise" players. They are so important to the organization that they have special terms and conditions placed in their contracts. Some software organizations reveal their rankings through job title. For example, some companies might use a designator in the job title such as Level I, Level II, Senior, or Principal. In both examples, the organizations used ranking as a way of dealing with important staffing issues.

How Employees Are Ranked

Ranking needs to be kept simple—you don't want to get carried away with the concept or let it dominate your time. I've found the simplest way to rank your employees is to assign each person to one of three levels: inner, middle, or outer circles.

The Inner Circle

Those employees who are most important to the company are put in the inner circle. Every good manager or leader will know who the most important contributors to the team are, and who they can count on when things get tough. You're truly building the product (and often the business) on these people. They are essential to your long-term success and must be recognized and rewarded accordingly.

The people assigned to the inner circle are typically your most senior, most talented, and most trusted team members. They are included in executive meetings about strategy, product direction, and other major company issues. They provide functional leadership and technical excellence; they can make the "big plays" when you need them most. They feel full responsibility for the product and are committed to its success. They have delivered for the team in the past, and they can and will do it again.

The Middle Circle

The middle circle is composed of the up-and-comers. These are the people who may not have all the talent or all the skills of the inner circle people, but are still very important to the success of the project. They typically have less experience than the inner circle, but have lots of enthusiasm, interest, growth potential, and attitude.

The middle circle is also where you find the people who perform well but who don't usually go above and beyond. They are steady, solid, and consistent, but not spectacular. The current version of the product is dependent on their abilities, but they are not currently franchise players.

The Outer Circle

The outer circle is composed largely of people who are new to the organization or who have not performed up to full expectations. New employees, no matter how promising, are still unknown and untried. They need to be given some time to work themselves into the core of the organization and prove their abilities to others.

The outer circle is composed of people who would be relatively easy to replace. If they were to leave the organization, it would not adversely impact the long-term success of the organization.

WHY RANKING IS USED

Ranking can help you decide how to allocate limited resources or assign new opportunities. It can also help you take care of the people who have contributed most to the organization's success and make sure that turnover does not come from the most important contributors to your development team. Let's discuss some of the important ways ranking can be used:

◆ *Recognizing contribution over time* Ranking allows people to be recognized for their contributions over time. If you have a superstar who has worked for the team for over five years, the fact that

he or she is part of the inner circle and being treated well is important not only to the individual but also to the other team members.
It shows that the organization recognizes the contribution, is thank-
ful for it, and is likely to recognize other people's contributions
over time as well.

◆ *Assigning perks or limited resources* When new perks and resources
appear that can't be shared by the entire team, who should get
them? With ranking, you have a pretty good idea. Whether it is
researching an exciting new technology, attending a trade show,
getting an office, or visiting a customer in Hawaii, you have an
ordered list of your contributors from which to start the selection
process.

Do the goodies always go to the inner circle members? No,
not necessarily. If your top-tier employees have all been taken care
of or if one particular perk means a lot more to someone else, it's
probably wise to let that person have it. It's important to spread
the perks around—people in the outer and middle circles should
get something once in a while, too. But the basic principle remains:
Take care of those who take care of the product.

◆ *Managing compensation* Ranking also helps you to plan salary
increases, bonus plans, and option allocations. Of course you
need to take the best care of the inner circle; they have delivered
for the organization and you need to let them know that they are
appreciated. Perhaps they are placed on a bonus plan or get stock
options—perhaps both. Whatever you decide to do, it's important
that you compensate them well and that they know their accomplishments are recognized.

The middle circle should get the next level of compensation
and the outer gets the last. Remember that "next" and "last" don't
necessarily mean compensation that is at or below market level.
You're not trying to punish the outer circle; you're just not rewarding them as much as the others. The fact that increased compensation programs are available for increased performance should
be an incentive.

◆ *Managing retention* A wise person once told me that when the
turnover winds blow, you can afford to lose a lot of leaves (outer
circle) because those can be grown back relatively quickly. But

you must avoid damage to the branches (middle circle) and the trunk (inner circle). Those are difficult to repair and take longer to grow back. The basic lesson is straightforward. If your turnover is coming from the inner circle or middle circles, you've got a serious problem that needs to be addressed. Ranking can help you understand where your turnover is occurring and the impact it has on your team.

How Not to Use Ranking

Be careful not to use ranking inappropriately. Don't use ranking to split teams apart or to create a "them vs. us" mentality. Beware of creating a "holier than thou" attitude in your teams as well. You don't want a feeling of superiority to get in the way of teamwork. If people start feeling overly important and do not recognize that everyone needs to contribute in order for everyone to win, you'll have all sorts of problems. Remember, it's important to recognize and reward someone's contribution without letting it cause jealousy or antagonism in the team.

What You Give, What You Get

With increased privileges come increased responsibilities. The old saying "To whom much is given, much is expected" is certainly true when it comes to ranking. Don't let the privileges of rank outweigh the responsibilities. Both

---

Back at Work

At NuMega, we half-jokingly referred to our engineering staff as gods, demi-gods, and gods-in-training. Everyone on the staff was at least good, and most were great, but not everyone made the same level of contribution to the organization.

Those who contributed more were given more opportunities and more freedom. But they were also counted on to deliver new features; to come up with breakthroughs; and to provide leadership, guidance, and advice to others when it was needed. Because most of our superstars were both talented and humble, there was seldom any grief when it came to recognizing their contributions.

---

privilege and responsibility should come in equal measure. If one gets more weight than the other, there can be a wide variety of subtle—and not so subtle—problems.

WHEN BEHAVIOR CHANGES

What happens when a member of the inner circle starts behaving like a member of the outer circle? Conversely, what happens when a new hire blows everyone away with his or her performance?

In the first scenario, the best approach is to discuss the issue with the person and present concrete details on the decline in performance. This discussion will often reveal the source of the problem. Is it burnout? A personal issue? Armed with this knowledge, you will have a chance to deal with the problem straight on.

In the second case, it appears you've found a superstar. First, it's important to make sure the performance is sustained. This knowledge usually takes a full release cycle; there is no need to rush to judgment. Superstars tend to be superstars not just once, but continually and repeatedly. If stand-out performance continues, then inner circle membership should be happily awarded.

WHAT YOU'RE AFTER

The ultimate goal, of course, is to bring everyone into the inner circle. The best thing that could happen would be to have a stable full of inner circle players. There should be no artificial limits on how many people can be part of the inner circle. Although a bell curve is typical, don't force a distribution pattern on your team. Let it be a true reflection of the actual team members' contribution.

CULTURE

Culture, as it applies to software development, involves the set of behaviors and beliefs that drive the software development process. A culture is created first by the principles and actions of the management and leadership of the organization. Over time, it grows either positively or negatively based on the team's past successes, failures, responses to problems, and ability to perform. These factors ultimately define the team's self-image. It can be anything from a top-flight engineering team that ships great products, to a team suffering from release to release and barely getting the job done.

WHY IS CULTURE SO IMPORTANT?

You must remember that like an individual, a team has an idea of its purpose, its importance, its talent level, and its ability to execute a task. If the ideas the team has of itself are positive, the team will be highly motivated and able to perform with very high levels of quality and productivity. Likewise, if the images are negative, the team will perform well below its capabilities—even if it is composed of talented people! In a sense, a culture can act as either an accelerator or a decelerator on the team's overall ability to perform.

For example, a good culture will be a tremendous asset when you need to take advantage of new opportunities or respond to difficult challenges. If you have a culture of shipping quality products, it's highly likely that there will be internal pressure and commitment to continue this practice.

On the other hand, a bad culture will only add more problems to an already difficult situation. For example, if there needs to be a quick response to an external event but the team has never had a culture of responding quickly, there will be a great deal of doubt that they will be successful or whether they should even try.

HOW CAN YOU BUILD YOUR CULTURE?

As mentioned previously, the best way to create and build your culture is to make sure you start with a commitment to certain principles and an expectation of certain behaviors. Then, everyone must perform well for a period of time. The actions taken by the team in pursuit of these principles are what form the group's culture.

Back at Work

We took specific, deliberate actions to build the culture at NuMega.

- *We clearly defined our identity and purpose.* We knew exactly who we were and what we needed to do. Sounds simple, doesn't it? But it can often be more complicated than it seems.

  We wanted to build the world's best development tools, particularly tools that helped developers debug or solve problems with their software. We knew that anything that this involved was within our scope. We wanted to understand it, adopt it, or do it better than anyone else.

- *We cultivated elitism.* Because of the talent we had and the selectivity of our hiring process, many people felt that it was a privilege to be a part of our engineering organization. Cultivating an environment of privilege kept morale high and turnover low. Elitism created a culture of confidence, of doing remarkable things, and of being part of something special.

  Remember, elitism is relative. If you compare your team's talent to the talent in other companies in your field, you need to have the top talent in the industry. But if you compare your team to other teams in your division of the company, then you simply need to have the top talent in your division—something that is probably easier to do. The benefits of elitism still apply.

- *We celebrated success and told our history.* Over time, we had a string of remarkable technical and product successes. The founders made sure they highlighted these technical successes at company meetings with informal speeches. Everyone made sure each new employee knew the company's history and progress. This encouraged a culture of winning, of building great products, and of being experts in our chosen area.

  The principle here is important. Your history impacts the formation of culture. Make sure you put a string of wins together to show what the team is capable of doing. Make sure you celebrate your success and tell your history.

◆   *We stoked the competitive fires.* To give the team a rallying point, we defined our competition clearly and targeted them as the enemy. We could then circle our wagons and aim outward, not inward. The focus on competition was heavily emphasized and permeated much of our discussions and thoughts. Sometimes, it overflowed in interesting ways, including some unusual competitive trade show stunts by the development team. All of this showed me that this team would do just about anything to win; we were building a great competitive culture.

◆   *We went out of our way to be different and have fun.* Two of the treats of being with an engineering-oriented company were the amount of fun we could have and the things we could get away with. We got tons of free stuff: t-shirts, trade show swag, and free lunches. The additions of hat day, "NuMega specials" (a pizza with caramelized onions, garlic, and red hot chili peppers), homemade indoor miniature golf courses, and indoor bicycle racing all created an atmosphere of being different and having fun. We knew that we were not typical and we reveled in it.

◆   *We put the dev team in front of customers.* NuMega strongly believed in getting members of the development team in front of customers. One of the most effective ways of doing this was to let dev team members staff the trade show booth. In addition to getting a break from work, they were on the front lines answering questions, getting ideas, and hearing the good and the bad about the products.

After a show, the morale was sky-high, and everyone had heard a consistent set of needs and priorities. There was a real connection between what we were building and the people who were using it.

Let's get a little more concrete. The first step in building a culture is defining what is most important to you. What does your culture value today? What would you like it to value? The following is a list to get you thinking. Does your team:

◆ Value on-time delivery?

◆ Value technical excellence?

◆ Value high quality?

◆ Value even the smallest contribution?

◆ Reward risk taking?

◆ Reward exceptional performance?

◆ Show generosity?

◆ Show concern for social issues?

◆ Believe that everyone should help to test the product?

◆ Respond quickly to external threats?

◆ Believe that usability testing is critical to your success?

◆ Expect to work overtime when you fall behind schedule?

The next step is to decide what actions you will take to form your culture. What pressures will you endure, what decisions will you make, what issues will you raise, and what confrontations will you create to develop the culture you want? Think about it and be prepared to follow through with your decision. Remember, a culture will happen whether you try to direct it or not.

CULTURE AND PROCESSES

Another aspect of culture is your team's attitude and support of internal processes. Some cultures have a lot of development processes; others have almost none. Young companies are often loath to introduce processes, while larger organizations need them to get any work done at all. As your group grows, think about how you are going to introduce new processes. What types of processes are needed and which can you do without? How are you going to draw the line between working just short of chaos and drowning in mind-numbing rules and regulations?

Here are some guidelines that might be helpful to you as your organization grows:

◆   *Analyze costs vs. benefits.* Recognize that adding processes is not inherently bad. It fact, sometimes it is absolutely necessary to getting work done. The trick is to make sure that each layer of process or each additional step adds more than it costs. This can sometimes be tough to know, but if there's doubt, then perhaps it shouldn't be done.

   If you feel that the addition of a new process is necessary, it is important to know how to introduce it to the team. A new process works best when it's clearly defined, has obvious benefits (provides real and perhaps measurable results), and is supported by the team. If the new process meets these criteria, it has a good chance of being used successfully.

   On the other hand, if the process doesn't have a solid definition, obvious value, or team support, you should question whether it's needed. This is not to say that it shouldn't be implemented, but you must be certain that its value is worth the cost. You must also be willing to work out the issues that will arise from its implementation. Don't be too quick to add processes, but don't hesitate to add them if you have a strong conviction that they are needed.

◆   *Follow the processes you have before adding new ones.* One of the most frustrating aspects of software development is watching the introduction of more processes when the team is not working well with the current ones. Don't let this happen to your team. Managers and leads are responsible for the team's correct execution of current processes. You will lose credibility with the team if you agree to add more processes when you are ignoring the ones you already have. If you find you've got a lot of documented processes that no one follows, call a meeting and decide with your team if those processes add value or not. If they do, keep them and follow them. If they don't, get rid of them. There's no point in having processes hung on the wall if no one is going to salute. It just cheapens the décor.

   The bottom line is this: Implement the minimum set of processes needed to get the job done and make sure the team executes them very, very well. Don't add new processes if you aren't committed to personally intervening when they aren't followed. The teams need to know that if you agree to do something, you're going to do it.

◆   *Weigh the needs of the many vs. the needs of the few or the one.* Processes are generally introduced to suit the needs of the whole team. But there are times when processes are suggested that will only help a few people or maybe even a single person. When this occurs, you have to be very careful about the cost/benefit analysis. If you're going to ask your whole team to do something extra, perhaps at significant cost, make sure the benefit to the few is worth the expense to the team. If it doesn't measure up, don't do it. If it does measure up, communicate the reasons to all of those affected and invest the time and energy necessary to make sure it's followed.

Back at Work

At NuMega, it was suggested that every bug we logged be accompanied by information about the hardware/software configuration of the PC on which that bug was found. The benefit to the person who suggested this would be the ability to track down certain types of bugs much easier. It was a great idea for environments that are diverse or that have distributed development teams. However, it would have been a real hassle for the rest of the team to manually enter this information accurately. We did not have a diverse environment, nor were we distributed in different physical locations.

Would it be of value? Yes, in some cases, perhaps five to ten bugs a month could be solved more easily if all the information was provided accurately. However, the cost of entering all this information by fifteen people during the internal development cycle (particularly when we logged perhaps ten issues a day) was not worth the benefit. Additionally, most of the bugs could be reproduced on any machine, and when this was not the case it was easy enough to go over to the submitter's office and ask for the configuration information needed.

By saying no to this suggestion, and many like it, we kept the process overhead low and our execution of necessary processes high.

COMMON PROBLEMS AND SOLUTIONS

The following are some of the typical problems and questions that surface when applying these techniques, and some solutions to those problems.

RANKING PROBLEMS

◆ *Keeping it a secret*   Don't hide the fact that employees are ranked. Although you don't need to hang a poster in the kitchen, you shouldn't cover up the fact that ranking exists and is used. It's important for people to know that their personal contribution is essential and that it is going to be evaluated and used for the allocation of perks and compensation.

◆ *Moving to higher or lower circles*   Don't put artificial barriers between the inner, middle, and outer circles. Contribution is the only way to move up into the higher circles, and the lack of contribution should be the only reason for moving down into the lower ones. Be sure to recognize someone's steady improvement from the outer circle to the middle circle—or someone's descent to the outer inner circle from the inner.

   As discussed earlier, when someone moves from one circle to another, be sure to discuss it with him or her. Moves in a positive direction should be recognized and rewarded. Moves in a negative direction should be recognized and privately discussed as well.

◆ *Playing favorites*   Don't let ranking be used or confused with personal favoritism. Ranking must be based only on contribution. If you have a personal friend on a team but he or she is not contributing as well as other members, your friend shouldn't get as many benefits as those who are contributing. Period. If you can't make this decision, you shouldn't be doing the ranking.

◆ *Fairness*   Some people might think that ranking isn't fair. This may be a result of prior experiences where ranking was not used appropriately. (See the discussion of favoritism above.) But in another respect, ranking really isn't fair—if fair means equal. Ranking is not about making things equal. Ranking is about allocating resources based on contribution and recognizing and providing incentives for great accomplishments. In a world of limited resources, you need a way to distribute benefits, and there is probably no better way than by ranking a person's contribution to his or her product or team.

CULTURE PROBLEMS

◆ *Change*   One of the biggest problems involving culture is the feeling that it can't be changed. This idea can seem particularly true in large groups or companies. Although a culture might be difficult to change, it's not impossible if the leadership is committed to making it happen. In addition, individual teams often have their own micro-culture within a larger company culture that can be changed with relative ease.

◆ *Growth*   As an organization grows, it is very important to communicate and share its culture with new employees. Startups in particular often experience very rapid growth and need to make sure they keep their core values intact. To do this, you must keep the following questions in mind:

  ◆ Who are we?

  ◆ What are we doing here?

  ◆ Why do we do it better than anyone else?

  ◆ What makes us special?

  ◆ What do we value?

Make sure that all current employees know the answers and that there is a mechanism in place to educate new employees. Whether it is a meeting with a member of the executive team or a discussion with the local team members, be sure to discuss your culture openly and with the seriousness that it deserves.

5

Software Tools

A t NuMega, we used only tools that were critical to our development effort and that could be molded to our way of working. Of all the tools that were available, the two that we used and relied on the most were a source code management system and an issue and problem management (bug tracking) system. The ability to mold or customize these products accelerated our development efforts; the entire team used them almost every day.

SOURCE CODE MANAGEMENT

Your source code is the second most important project asset—after your people of course. Consequently, all software projects, even those involving just a single person, must be able to maintain the integrity of their source code. Over the course of the development cycle, you will need to control, update, audit, and review changes to the source code. As the number of people who work on your project increases and the complexity of your project grows, these requirements become even more critical. Let's look at the fundamentals of source code management software and discuss some simple techniques to maximize its value.

WHAT IS IT?

Source code management products store code files, track versions, manage the files that compose a software development project, and provide the following functions:

◆ *Store a file and its past, present, and future versions.* The source code management system will maintain all versions of a file placed under its control. It will allow you to retrieve any version of the file that has been placed into the system. This feature is essential if you are going to build on prior versions or, even more importantly, build concurrent versions of the software.

◆ *Maintain the history of the changes to each file.* With each change to a file, the source code management system will maintain the history of the changes, including the date, time, user, and usually some text that the user enters describing the nature and scope of the change. Often these comments are the only information you might have. (This information can really help new developers come up to speed.)

◆   *Group related files.* As projects grow in complexity, it becomes necessary to group files by purpose. For example, you could group files by sub-projects or sub-systems. You could also group files by function—test beds, specifications, and documentation, for example.

◆   *Label files that are associated with a specific release of the software.* The source code management system will allow the user to place a label or a tag on specific versions of files across an entire project or sub-project. This critical ability allows you to permanently mark or identify the files that constitute a specific release of the software.

◆   *Lock and unlock files.* During the course of development, more than one individual will need access to a common set of files. If a file is not in use by someone else, source code management systems allow a user to lock the file and check the file out. This action will prevent any other user from modifying and potentially corrupting the file. When the user who checked the file out is finished and has checked the file back in, the system will unlock the file and allow another user to access and check it out. At times it might be critical for two developers to edit the same file at the same time. When this occurs, you can override the locks placed on the file, but it will then be up to you to coordinate the changes. Most sophisticated source code management products will support multiple checkouts by automatically merging the changes made between the two files. However, this can be dangerous, and most development teams perform a manual (user-controlled) merge operation instead.

What Goes in It?

One of the most frustrating (but avoidable) headaches of software development is locating all the files and information associated with a project. At NuMega, we didn't have time to create large infrastructures or processes to support a robust document management solution, so we decided simply to place all of our project related files and documents in the source code management system. These included:

- Source files
- Header files
- Libraries files
- Build scripts
- Compiler images
- Linker images
- Installation tools and files
- Testing tools and files
- Project specifications
- Project plans (software, documentation, and testing)
- User documentation
- QA's test scripts and test beds
- Developers' unit tests

Back at Work

Although we thought we were putting all essential files into the source code management system, we forgot one set of files: the developers' unit tests. The unit tests were short programs written by developers to test the functionality of the product. They would run these programs during development to make sure the software still worked. The unit tests were especially useful when the teams were updating features or fixing bugs. Some veteran developers also had dozens of little programs that checked for specific conditions and had special test cases that were never part of our formal test plans. It was a shame that these files weren't shared with others. If we had kept these tests in a central location like the source code management system, we could have run them automatically as part of our full QA test suite. In addition, these tests could have mitigated the risk of introducing new bugs by inexperienced developers working on fragile or complex portions of the code.

Notice that we put virtually everything into the source code management system—not just source code. If it was used or related to the project, we placed it in the system.

WHY DO IT?

There are major benefits to putting all the project files into the source code management system. First, no matter what file it is or when you joined the project, the chances are pretty good that you will be able to find the file in the source code management system. The ability to find key files under almost any circumstances can be extremely valuable. A developer can find test plans, a tech writer can find functional specifications, and a new hire can find all of the information he or she needs without any prior knowledge of the project history. Second, storing all project-related files in the source code management system extends the benefits of labeling, locking, revisions management, and history to the rest of the team.

For example, at NuMega, we were able to track changes to plans, test scripts, and documentation throughout the project. In addition, we were able to mark and label the entire set of test scripts and user documentation for every internal milestone and every minor or major release. We literally could re-create all the files—not just the source code—for any release in the project's history.

Of particular note is the inclusion in the NuMega system of the build tools: compilers, linkers, headers, and so on. Keeping these under control was critical to maintaining a consistent build environment across the project. The official build environment was always available in the source code management system; our developers *and* our build machines were required to pull the same set of files to build the software. No exceptions.

Because we didn't rely on any local files to build the software (other than the version control software), we maintained an identical build environment across the project. This simple concept saved us a lot of time. Prior to using this system, we were regularly chasing down build problems due to compiler incompatibilities between developers, or searching for hard-to-find run time errors caused by mismatched libraries or headers.

One final benefit—and it proved to be very valuable for us—was that the centralization of files into one source code management system allowed for easy backups of the project. With a single command, we were able to back up (or simply copy) the entire project to another drive or another machine.

WHAT ARE ITS PROCESS CAPABILITIES?

Besides the operational benefits described above, the NuMega teams needed to support five critical process capabilities. Although these were specific to our products and company, many are common to the majority of projects in the industry. These include:

- Managing the development of multiple product editions.

- Managing the development of multiple, concurrent releases (for each edition).

- Enabling and supporting the use of shared components, both within a single product and between other products in the company.

- Supporting the build of the product for the latest set of sources (or for some other specific set of sources).

- Supporting local developer builds.

HOW DO YOU MANAGE IT?

One of the greatest challenges in managing a software development project is keeping the complexity of the project under control. Source code and configuration management are certainly two of the toughest elements to handle. Although we did not find the silver bullet for these problems, our solution was workable and helped us ship on time without too many problems.

Our source code management system was Microsoft's Visual Source Safe (VSS). It provided the basic functionality we needed and had a great price—just right for a startup. Although a discussion of VSS is beyond the scope of this book, the following is an overview on how we utilized the product for our needs.

Structure Concepts

Our projects were structured on two very simple concepts: parts and products. A *part* was a component used to build the software *product*. Parts could be owned by developers who were not members of our project team and who updated their parts on a different (but coordinated) development schedule than our projects. A product was the final package that was sold to customers. It was composed of parts and files unique to the product itself. By knitting together parts and products we were able to build different editions of our products, offer entirely new products, and still support concurrent development streams. For example, the ability to make bug fixes or service packs while continuing with a large development effort on a new code base was essential for both customer support and generating new revenue.

Source Pool Structures and Usage

All the files that were involved in our product development effort were categorized into these three folders:

◆   Product Name, for product-related files

◆   Environment, for development environment files

◆   Imports, for third-party files

The Product Name folder contained all the files that we supplied and that were required to build, test, or document the product. We had subfolders named Branch for each variant we were working on. We had another subfolder named Parts for the common and shared components that contributed to the product. Finally, we had subfolders named Products for each edition of the product. Each Product subfolder included the parts it needed. To make this work, a consistent naming convention and structure was important. Coordinating changes between parts and products was critical as well.

Back at Work

When I first started at NuMega, one of our products had three directories for the source code, all based on the names of the developers: Frank, Bill, and Matt. Because each person worked on his own code, they were able to manage changes without corruption. However, there was little common source code (usually just one big data structure in which all information was passed between major sub-systems). Hey—it worked. But we needed to increase the size of the team and the development effort, and we couldn't do it without a source code management system. The benefits and capabilities of a source code management system allowed us to grow in sophistication and manage complexity over time. I simply can't see developing software without one.

Table 5-1 shows a generic template for the structure of the Product Name folder.

TABLE 5-1   SAMPLE STRUCTURE FOR PRODUCT NAME FOLDER

File Name and Level	Contents
$/Product Name	Files specific to the product
Branch	Variant streams of development
Parts	Shared files that contribute to the product
Src	Source code for the Parts (shared as needed with /Products/Src)
Doc	Doc file sources
Help	Help file sources
Install	Install procedure source code
Patch	Patch source code
Setup	Setup source code
Samples	Sample source code
Tests	Test source code, test beds, and so on
Product	Editions of the Product Name (one per edition)
Output	Output area for software built under other projects
Src	Source code for the product (shared as needed with /Parts/Src)
Doc	Product doc files (shared from /Parts/Doc)
Help	Product help files (shared from /Parts/Help)
Imports	Imports (shared from $/Imports)
Install	Product installation files (shared from /Parts/Install)
Samples	Product samples (shared from /Parts/Samples)
Tests	Test beds, test suites (shared from /Parts/Test)

The Environment ($/Env) folder stored the files that supported the product development effort but that were not part of the final product. These included everything from tools and utilities to coding standards and project templates. The Environment folder contained the environment files, which described the environment from a development point of view, as well as from a testing, documentation, and human factors point of view. At NuMega, because we wanted our development environments to be shared between product teams, we created a specific section of the source pool dedicated to this need. Table 5-2 is a sample list of the subfolders that could appear in this part of the source pool.

TABLE 5-2   SAMPLE STRUCTURE FOR ENVIRONMENT FOLDER

File Name and Level	Contents
$/Env	
Dev	Environment software and dev tools
Bin	Binaries for these tools (subfolder for each)
Src	Source for these tools (subfolder for each)
Doc	Doc for these tools (sub folder for each)
Etc	Miscellaneous files not categorized above (lint libraries)
Test	Environment tools and files for testing
Bin	Binaries for these tools
Src	Source and doc for these tools
Doc	Documentation on the test environment
Etc	Miscellaneous files not categorized above
Documentation	Documentation on the project environment
Templates	Project templates, writing templates, and style guides
Plans	Project, QA, and doc plans and specs
Process	Process documents for the project
Etc	Miscellaneous files not categorized above

The Imports ($/Imports) folder stored the files or tool kits from third-party products. The third-party product itself was not stored in the $/Imports folder, just the libraries and headers. As a result, there weren't many changes to the Imports section of the source pool. However, because this area was used to store versions of the product, it was very important not to introduce changes without careful thought, testing, and communication with the parties who might be affected. Labeling was key to maintaining version consistency over time. Table 5-3 is a sample list of the subfolders for $/Imports.

TABLE 5-3   SAMPLE STRUCTURE FOR IMPORTS FOLDER

File Name and Level	Contents
$/Imports	
RogueWave	RogueWave libraries, headers
ObjectSpace	Object space libraries, headers
Visual C	Visual C compiler images, libraries, headers
Install Shield	Install Shield libraries, headers
[More]	Folder for each third-party tool or library

The Build System

At NuMega, we wrote a script to build the product on a dedicated "build machine." The script would pull the files needed to build the product from the source code management system. This information would include the build tools themselves as well as the sources, libraries, headers, and other required files. Nmake, a popular build management tool, was used to drive the compilation of the product. Nmake would first build all the product's parts and then build the final product binaries themselves.

The build script took a build label as input, which allowed us to build a specific version of the software. Because we labeled and selected both the build tools and the product files, we were guaranteed a consistent build environment. The build scripts also used common environment variables and macros so that we could build all parts and products with a single invocation. The fact that our build machines and our developers were using the same build scripts, build tools, and build environments allowed any developer to build the project easily and consistently.

Having an automated, rock-solid build system is an essential key to successful development. It's well worth the time and effort to get this done up front. This and other release engineering topics are covered in Chapter 7.

Issue and Problem Management

Software development is a dynamic and communication-intensive process. As a team works on a project, it's very important to have formal ways of managing and resolving the problems, issues, and bugs that arise. An issue and problem management product is one of the best ways to address this critical need. The remainder of this chapter explains how you can effectively use such a product.

What Is It?

Issue and problem management software allows product teams to manage the seemingly endless number of issues and problems that surface during the project development effort. It allows team members to log, update, assign, prioritize, categorize, and review all the information that has been entered over the course of the development project. It is an essential part of any development project, regardless of size. No one person can remember in complete detail all of the issues and problems that need to be resolved. If they are not logged, reviewed, prioritized, and closed, your development team will suffer untold communication and quality nightmares.

What Goes in It?

At NuMega, we used the issue and problem management system to store virtually all soft or transient data about the project. This included all software bugs—including functional, performance, installation and setup, and all build bugs—and solutions or suggestions to improve the project in both

---

Note

 I wouldn't recommend writing your own issue and problem management software because there are a variety of commercial software solutions available at affordable prices. These include Compuware / NuMega's TrackRecord, PVCS Tracker, Rational ClearQuest, and others. Although you'll need to do your own research on which one meets your needs, I strongly suggest that the make vs. buy decision is weighted toward buy. You don't need to spend your time creating tools; you need to ship your software.

---

the current and future releases. The principle here is very simple and very important: You must keep all this data in a single repository. Don't keep this information in anything that cannot be shared, backed up, and made easily accessible. (This rules out e-mail messages!)

Consider this example. A developer notices that performance on some portion of the application has really slowed down and sends an e-mail message to the team distribution list. What happens next? Some people might look at it, but others might not. Even if someone addresses the issue, it still needs to be logged and closed out; otherwise it is likely to be forgotten. Sending the e-mail message is not a bad thing, but not logging the issue in the system is a problem. The same thing applies to suggestions for the current release. If an e-mail message is sent out without logging the suggestion as well, there's a possibility that no one will follow up, and it's unlikely that there will be any history as to how or if the suggestion was applied.

How Does It Work?

Given the discussion above, it's important to understand how to automate the basic information flow between team members. Remember, the tool should work for you and not the other way around. You need to manage

---

Back at Work

When I started at NuMega, bugs and various other issues were tracked on a white board—if they were tracked at all. Those bugs and issues stayed on the white board until they were resolved, and then they were simply erased. When the board got too full, a new entry was jammed into a corner or some other issue was erased to make room. That system worked for one or two people, but the history of those bugs and other issues was nonexistent. When the organization began to grow, it became obvious that we needed an automated solution. If we hadn't made this transition at that time, we would not have been able to grow the engineering group with any degree of success. Although finding the tool that would solve our problem was not difficult, how we used that tool was often the subject of much debate. However, we eventually discovered that for a group our size, it was more important to execute a few things really well than to attempt to do everything we could think of.

information easily and without a great deal of overhead. At the same time, you need to make sure you maintain engineering discipline and do not get sloppy. You can use the issue and problem management system to do this. Configure the system to capture the following basic project data:

◆ The current state of the problem—open or closed

◆ The date created, updated, and closed

◆ A text description of the problem

◆ The release number/build number of the software exhibiting the problem

◆ The name of the person who submitted the problem

◆ The name of the person who currently owns the problem

◆ The status of the problem—under investigation, need more info, waiting on external event, fixed, and the like

◆ The priority of the problem—low, medium, high

◆ The release in which the problem exists

◆ The status of QA verification

◆ The number of times the problem's fix has failed

◆ The list of changes to the issue or problem report

Let's take a look at how we used the issue and problem management software at NuMega.

Have One Source for Bugs and Issues

We had a very simple rule: All bugs and issues were logged into the bug tracking system. If they were not there, they didn't exist. This simplified our issue management activities enormously. Rumors, talk in the hallways, and e-mail were not valid means of logging bugs. For example, if an issue came in from technical support, product management, sales support—whoever— it was not an officially recognized issue until it was logged. As we grew, technical support took on more of the work of logging bugs on behalf of external groups, but the idea remained the same.

How far does this go? Does this mean that if one developer has a problem with another developer's implementation of some APIs, he needs to log it? No, not necessarily. The developers might be able to work out this issue one on one, and it will never need to be logged. However, if the issue is something that is going to take time and needs to be tracked (that is, it's really important), it makes more sense to log it and have some documentation justifying its existence so that it's not forgotten. The same concept applies to any member of the team and any department.

Another benefit of logging issues is having the ability to report on them. Wouldn't it be great to go to a status meeting and have a complete list of all major issues and their owners easily available? This is an efficient way to drive an agenda and keep the important questions front and center during the development process. The submitter will really appreciate that his issues are being recognized and discussed. The people assigned to their resolution will also realize they can't duck the issues forever.

Manage Change

As mentioned at the beginning of this section, you can implement a change management process by using the issue and problem management system. Because all serious concerns are logged, you can easily pull up a list of the changes that need to be considered. After a decision is made about an issue, simply update the issue's history with the resolution. The ability to review past decisions and the reasons they were made is a big benefit and should eliminate the "I can't remember" or "I must have missed that meeting" excuses. It's simple, it's clean, and it allows a great deal of control.

Use Time-Based Prioritization

Although classifications like low, medium, and high are often useful in categorizing issues, they still can leave you with dozens or even hundreds of issues all in the same category. What is missing is an associated time element to the prioritization. It's very common to have high priority bugs that need to be fixed for a beta but other high priority bugs that can wait until the last release because of their complexity or the need for more investigation.

Consider using the Fixed For field for time-based prioritization. The values placed in this field can be based on the internal release schedule of the project, such as a specific milestone, beta stage, or release candidate. Ask yourself these kinds of questions to help establish priorities: "Does this problem have to be resolved at milestone 2, or can it wait until beta 1?" " What happens if we release the product now and fix this bug in the next edition?"

As you progress through the development cycle, you can assign specific issues to be fixed for specific internal development milestones. Doing so makes it very easy to see the current list of issues for any given release, including the next one.

Verify and Fix Bugs

One of the important tasks that QA performs is verifying that bugs are actually fixed in the software. This step makes sure that the developer really understood the problem and tested it well. When a bug is fixed and checked back into the sources, the developer sets the QA Verify field to True and the status to Pending QA Verify. After QA has verified the bug, the QA engineer sets the state of the bug to Closed. Only QA can close out a bug, and QA does so only after it has been verified.

Include a Release Note

At NuMega, when we came across an issue that needed to be part of the release notes or Read Me file, we would change its status to Release Note but would keep it open. Release notes described known issues, workarounds, and late-breaking information that didn't make it into the formal documentation. When the end of the beta or final release came, it was very easy to call up the issues we believed were candidates for a release note. Only after the issue was addressed and taken care of did we finally consider that issue closed.

Use Common Queries

It's very important to have a set of common queries for the project that search the database in a consistent manner. These queries must be shared and available to all team members; it's important that everyone has the same view of the data. Although personal queries are fine for infrequent or specialized reporting needs, you don't want your team using them for their work assignments. The risk of the queries being improperly defined or working off obsolete fields is quite high. The table on the following page shows the most important queries.

Query	Result
All open bugs	Allows the project manager and leads to assess the overall project
All open bugs with a fix for = "milestone value"	Allows the team to see what bugs remain open project-wide for a given milestone
All open bugs with owner = "owner value"	Allows an individual to see his or her current bug list
All open bugs with owner = "owner value" and fix for = "milestone value"	Allows an individual to see his or her bug list for a given milestone
All open bugs with QA verify = "true"	Allows QA team to see their QA verify list
All open bugs with suggestion = "true"	Allows project manager and leads to review current requests for changes

WHAT ARE ITS ADVANCED USES?

The following are some other important uses for the information that is being captured in the issue and problem database. This information can help the project manager and the leads understand some of the macro-level activity on the project as well as other specific problems that are eating up precious time. Remember, your team is processing hundreds and probably thousands of issues and bugs over the course of the development cycle, so having an understanding of what is happening over time can be very valuable.

Open Rates and Closure Rates

Open rates are a measure of how many new bugs or issues are being logged over a period of time. Open rates spike at the beginning of a project but should drop as time goes on. Closure rates are a measure of how many existing bugs or issues are being closed out. Closure rates should fall as bugs and issues are addressed. Figures 5-1 and 5-2 illustrate open rates and closure rates for a project—data that can be extremely useful.

One question to ask is, "How does the open rate compare to the closure rate?" At the beginning of the project, you're going to see a lot of new problems being opened faster than you can close them. As the project moves forward, the open rate vs. the closure rate should stop growing and level off as existing issues are closed more quickly than new ones are opened. Sharp spikes over prolonged periods of time should be investigated. Look at the details of problems logged over that period to see if there's a bigger set of issues emerging.

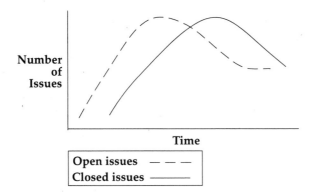

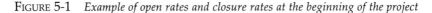

FIGURE 5-1   *Example of open rates and closure rates at the beginning of the project*

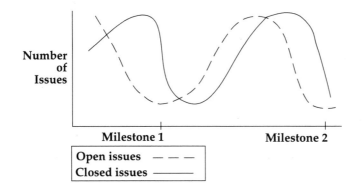

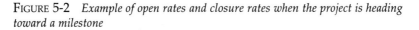

FIGURE 5-2   *Example of open rates and closure rates when the project is heading toward a milestone*

You should see your closure rate rise above your open rate as you head toward internal milestones, completion dates, betas, and certainly release candidates. If it's not, you're adding more new problems than you're solving—not a situation you want to see when heading into a period of stability or release.

The closure rate will also help you estimate how effectively the team can address issues and how much time it might take to close future issues. For example, if your closure rate has been ten bugs a day for the last two weeks, that might be great progress. If you have 100 outstanding bugs you could reasonably expect to close all the bugs in about ten days. This figure is not exact of course—one bug could take weeks to solve—but it allows you to have some idea of what you might expect when you have a large number of outstanding bugs.

Change Rates

Change rates can also be very telling. A change rate measures how many times the same issue has been updated. The reason for the update doesn't matter. A high change rate is a sure sign that things aren't running smoothly. For example, an open bug can often get passed around to many different people over a period of time and not be addressed by any of them. Perhaps it's being passed between development and tech support, between QA and development, or between two developers over and over again. Watching the change rates on bugs can help identify issues that need attention from leads and project manager.

Fix Failed Counts

Another good way of measuring vibration in the project is to maintain a "fix failed" count for each bug that was supposed to be fixed but wasn't. Fixing a bug requires the QA team to verify that the bug is actually closed. If the problem still exists or if the fix has not been verified, the status of the bug is set back to open, and the Fix Failed field is set to 1. If the QA team continues to be unable to verify that the bug has been fixed and the fix failed count rises to 2 or 3, this signals a problem, and the leads or project manager should get involved.

ADVANCED TOOLS

Although the source code management and issues and problem management tools were the backbone of NuMega's development process, we also used several other tools regularly throughout the development process.

DEBUGGERS

One of the most important tools for our developers was a debugger called SoftICE (a tool developed by NuMega Technologies). SoftICE is an incredibly powerful Windows debugger. It loads at system startup as a kernel level device driver and allows for unprecedented control and visibility into the internals of the application and the operating system. The development team frequently used SoftICE to solve some of our toughest debugging problems.

PERFORMANCE ANALYSIS AND COVERAGE ANALYSIS TOOLS

We frequently used performance analysis tools, including our own TrueTime and TrueCoverage products, to tune the performance of the applications we were building. We found that these tools should be used regularly during the development cycle and not at the end when there's no time left for optimizations or fixing problems. Analyzing the performance of a project at milestone and beta releases anticipates problems and can often uncover design issues that would have lurked in the code until release. Don't wait until you have a performance problem to start using a performance analysis tool.

We also found that these tools worked best when we built our project specifically for performance or coverage analysis. When we created these builds, we could integrate them with our test bed to find performance problems earlier or to better evaluate the coverage of our test bed.

SCRIPTING AND TEST AUTOMATION TOOLS

Because our QA plans called for as much automation as possible, we were always interested in tools that could help us in this regard. Some of the most

---

Back at Work

When we first established our code coverage development team, the members weren't exactly confident that code coverage was a real value. But as the project wore on and the team started to use their own product on their own code, it became clear that if developers unit-tested their code to an 80 percent coverage level, the quality of the product increased dramatically.

---

important were scripting tools (Perl, DOS batch files, and the like) and test automation tools. At the time, Visual Test was available for a good price and was marketed to sophisticated QA teams and developers. We used it for UI testing but relied on the scripting tools for the vast majority of our automation.

Common Problems and Solutions

The following are some of the typical problems and questions that surface when applying these techniques, and some solutions to those problems.

Tool Problems

◆ *Getting the tools you need*   One of the biggest mistakes a development team can make is not having the appropriate tools to support their development effort. I certainly believe that source code management and issue and problem management are essential. I would also argue that debugging, error-detection, performance, and coverage tools are equally important to a development team to help them solve the many unique problems that surface during the course of development.

Anything you can do to accelerate and automate the development cycle is critical to your schedule. Too often, schedules are blown because difficult bugs or performance problems are introduced during development and are not detected early enough. When they are detected, it's nearly impossible for people to solve them without help. This is no time to start looking around the Internet for tools. Be sure you have already evaluated which tools you need, integrated them into your development process, and trained your staff on their use.

◆ *Changing tools mid-stream*   One of the biggest temptations in the course of a development cycle is to replace what you're using now with a new version or a new vendor's tool. The consequences of this decision are usually significantly underestimated. I can't see changing source code management or issue and problem management systems without a major slip in the schedule. It's usually better to get through the release with what you have than to change in the middle.

SOURCE CODE MANAGEMENT PROBLEMS

◆   *Project structure*   As a project grows, the structure of the source code management tool will become very important. Although I discuss a common way of handling this issue, don't forget to plan for the specific needs of your project. You must consider the impact of simultaneous releases (service packs, minor releases, and major releases) and the needs of development, QA, user education, human factors, and release engineering.

◆   *Content*   Don't fool yourself into thinking that source code is the only set of files that needs change control. As I mentioned above, a wide range of documents and files need to be managed—don't limit the benefits of change control to just the source code. Even if you have to train your QA or user education staff on the use of a source code management tool, you'll find it well worth the time.

Back at Work

We once had a team that evaluated their new bug tracking system during development. They decided, after spending some time with it, that they should switch over to the new product because it had some neat new features. They ran the conversion utility, loaded it up, and starting using it. Unfortunately, about a week or so into the product's use, they found that the product didn't support some of their basic reporting needs, and the performance was terrible. They needed to go back to the previous system, but because there was no automated conversion, they had to re-enter—by hand—all the bugs and issues logged since the original conversion.

◆ *Contention over key files*   The typical scenario is developer X has
checked out a file, so developer Y can't check it out to make critical changes. This type of contention for files can really slow down
a project. You must have a way for critical bug fixes or changes
to be made quickly.

The best way to solve this problem is to avoid it. See if you
can divide the most popular content into more files based on logical sub-systems, components, and classes. Decomposing the
files' contents makes it less likely that there will be contention.

When it doesn't make sense to divide the content any further because of the tight coupling of the information, you should
develop a policy that requires files to be checked back in within
a certain number of hours after checkout. Developers can also
work on copies rather than on the actual file while it is unavail-
able. When the file is available, it can be checked out for a short
period of time, quickly updated, and checked back in.

Most source code management systems support a merge
feature. This allows you to combine changes made to the files you
want to check in with the copy that is already present in the
system. Although this is fine in most cases, don't let the merge
operation happen automatically—you want to make sure you
review each and every change made to the file. If your source
code management system has poor merge support, code editors
like Visual Slick Edit and Code Write allow you to see the differences visually and review each merge before it's made.

◆ *Labeling*   One of the greatest benefits of a source code management system is its ability to label a set of files that were involved
in a release. Don't forget to do this very simple step for each
release, including base levels, milestones, betas, and so on.

The labels should include more than just the source code
files. Include build files, installation files, documentation files,
QA files—all the files involved in the release. The label should be
descriptive and follow a project-specific naming convention.

ISSUE AND PROBLEM MANAGEMENT PROBLEMS

◆   *Data integrity*   The integrity of the data in your system must be
a priority. If you can't trust the information in the system, you
won't use it, and it will be of little value. It's very important that
you define data integrity rules, largely based on your internal
development process. For example, you should never see a bug
that is "closed" with a status of "under investigation." The status needs to be changed to reflect some form of resolution. Also,
make sure you update the fields with the appropriate status values (milestone information, release information, and so on).
Whatever your internal consistency checks are, don't let your data
get stale or out of date, or the team will simply assign any value
and the entire system will become suspect and possibly useless.

I have shown you some ways to model the key parts of your
development cycle using issue and problem management tools.
However, don't get carried away and try to model everything that
goes on with your team. Instead, you want to identify the key information needs of your development process and define some simple
fields and processes to support it.

The best way to avoid data integrity problems is to make
sure the team understands the importance of the data and can
detect and fix problems themselves. Self-enforcement works well
when you can demonstrate the data's real value to the team. In
addition, be sure to review the data periodically and discuss the
results with the team.

I have shown you some ways to model the key parts of your
development cycle using issue and problem management tools.
However, don't get carried away and try to model everything that
goes on with your team. Instead, you want to identify the key information needs of your development process and define some simple
fields and processes to support it.

6
Fundamentals of Quality Assurance

Quality assurance (QA) problems can ruin projects. They can render your schedule meaningless or make the product unacceptable to customers. Whether you're a startup or a multinational corporation, you need to effectively balance the quality of your product and the time it takes to get that product to market. It could very well mean the difference between success and failure.

This chapter discusses the essentials of QA in a fast-paced, resource-starved environment—the typical environment for almost all of today's software projects. I focus on critical QA-related concepts: what to test, how and when to test it, and who should test it. Then I show a single solution that unites all the concepts, and discuss some simple and effective techniques for managing the testing process.

PHILOSOPHY

Let's start by looking at the principles that will guide your QA effort. The overriding theme is building quality into the product as it's being developed. Quality can't be added later—not without great cost, effort, and time delays. Building quality into the product is based on four simple concepts:

- Test the product in parallel with its development.

- Stabilize the product's quality at regularly scheduled milestones.

- Automate as much of the testing as possible.

- Ensure that your teams, processes, and culture value quality.

TESTING IN PARALLEL

In a time-pressured environment, it is absolutely crucial to find and fix problems as soon as they occur. The earlier you know about a problem, the quicker you can begin solving it. Your goal is to test features as soon as they are completed. This process is called testing in parallel. To properly test in parallel, you must have automated test beds or manual testing resources available the moment a new feature is completed. If a feature is scheduled to be complete by the end of week five, your QA team must be ready to test it during week six. This rule holds for all major features. Although it's preferable to have automated tests, if it is time to test a feature, you should be prepared to do it manually.

Table 6-1 is an ideal timeline for testing a set of features in parallel. Note how development and testing are tied as closely together as possible. When a feature is completed at the end of the week, the QA team is ready to start testing it at the beginning of the next week. Although developers are responsible for coding and unit testing, the QA team exercises the feature as thoroughly as possible in the time allowed. Because developers and QA must work together on a feature, they are collectively called a "feature team."

TABLE 6-1 FEATURE TEAM TIMELINE FOR FEATURES **A, B,** AND **C**

	Purpose	**Development Schedule**	**QA Schedule**
Week 1	Develop	Code feature A	Test planning for features A and B
Week 2	Develop	Complete feature A	Test planning for features A and B
Week 3	Develop	Code feature B	Test feature A
Week 4	Develop	Complete feature B	Test feature A (or test planning for feature B)
Week 5	Develop	Code feature C	Test feature B
Week 6	Stabilize	Test and fix problems with features A and B	Test features A and B
Week 7	Stabilize	Test and fix problems with features A and B	Test features A and B together
Week 8	Develop	Complete feature C	Test planning for feature C

Developers and QA engineers are jointly responsible for delivering quality features on time. In this system, a feature is not done when it is coded. It's done when it's been tested by the QA team and meets certain criteria. The developers and QA engineers must recognize that they need to work together to get the feature done. Both have their own deliverables (coding, testing, automation, and the like), but it's only by working together that they get the entire job done. In fact, they shouldn't move on to the next feature until they have delivered and stabilized the current feature set.

Bear in mind that you should not have more features in development than you can staff with feature teams. In other words, the number of feature teams should be based on the number of features you can afford to work on in parallel—in both development and QA. If you find you have more QA engineers than developers or vice versa, you have an unbalanced team for this development model and need to recruit in the area where you're understaffed.

Finally, note that I have built a stabilization and integration period into the schedule. Stabilization and integration periods provide the team with a chance to solidify the software at key milestones before continuing on with the rest of the project. I'll discuss the need for stabilization and integration periods in the next section. I'll also discuss how to build stabilization periods into your schedule in Chapter 11.

STABILIZATION AND INTEGRATION

Every four to six weeks, the team should spend a week or two (depending on the complexity of the project) focused on testing, stabilizing, and integrating the features that are completed at that point. These periods of stabilization and integration help the team, the features, and the quality get in sync. During this time period, you can catch up on any testing that hasn't been completed, begin testing integrated features, and address issues that need resolution before the project continues. Don't be overly concerned with minor bugs or fine details; just make sure that the project is structurally and functionally sound before you continue with the next leg of the project. Everyone on the team should be focused on this stabilization and integration effort during this period. Don't work on new features, new code, or anything else until you're sure you have stabilized what you have already built.

Stabilization and integration periods are also opportunities to measure your actual progress against your scheduled progress. If you've scheduled your project well, you'll know on which week each of the features should be complete. Are you on schedule? Can you use these features on that date? This is crucial information for keeping the project on track. Again, I'll discuss creating and sticking to a project schedule in detail in Chapter 11, but for now just bear in mind that you want to have predefined periods in which the entire project team will focus on stabilizing the software.

AUTOMATION

One of the keys to testing in parallel (and finding bugs earlier) is automating as much of the testing as possible. Automation will provide you with the following significant benefits:

◆ *Reducing your internal testing cycle*   Automation helps you perform your tests quickly. To test in parallel, you need to be able to test a large amount of the product in a short amount of time continually throughout the development cycle. Manual testing is slow, labor intensive, and error prone. It can't be done every night on the latest development build. Automation is the only way you can get the most from testing in parallel.

◆ *Reducing your labor and staffing needs*   Automation of testing procedures can greatly reduce labor costs. Once in place, the relative cost of executing the automated test beds is a fraction of the cost of executing them manually.

◆ *Verifying changes made late in the development cycle*   Although last minute changes might be unavoidable, having solid automated test beds is crucial to quickly verifying that no significant problems were introduced by the changes. It's very costly—and nearly impossible—to manually execute all the tests that a few changes can require.

◆ *Providing test coverage for releases over time*   With each new release, the team must be certain that the features from prior releases still work. If you have to manually test the entire feature set from the older release all over again, you may not have enough resources to test the new features as well. Over time, the amount of manual testing that needs to be done can get overwhelming. Automating the testing of features from prior releases can solve this problem.

Back at Work

Once, after giving an update on the progress of a project to my boss and assuring him that everything was OK, I installed the daily build and pressed the "do the most critical feature of this product" button. It didn't work. I learned that the daily build was broken and had been for many days, although most of the team didn't know it. We were well past developing and testing this feature in our schedule, and it should have been, as it once was, rock solid. We realized that if the most critical feature of the product wasn't stable, the status of other features that had been functional in past builds was largely unknown as well. Everyone had been so busy writing new code or testing new secondary features that no one noticed that the product wasn't working anymore. And beta was just weeks away.

At that point the team and I realized how important test automation was to our project. We began writing and running automated regression tests for key features every day and fixing serious problem immediately.

One of the common criticisms of test automation is the amount of time it takes to create good test beds. Although it is true that there is an up-front time and labor cost, if the test beds are done well, they will pay big dividends later. I recommend having dedicated automation engineers whose only job is to write automated test beds throughout the development cycle.

The amount of maintenance required to keep automation relevant for future releases is also subject to some criticism. This is especially true for UI test automation. If your UI tends to have major changes between releases, the test scripts can break and require a lot of effort to update. For this reason, automation efforts should be focused on the non-UI features of a product. Focus the automation on the core features—not on the bells and whistles, and not on the minutiae of the user interface.

It's also a great idea to build a product with "testability" in mind. If you can minimize your dependence on the UI and create alternative ways to supply input and review output, you'll be shielded from changes in the UI. For example, consider using files, registry entries, command line parameters, and COM interfaces for input. Consider using text files, print statements, or off-the-shelf components for output. I'm not suggesting that the UI not be tested, but the priority for automated tests should be the core feature set of the product. If you are ready to do automated UI testing, however, consider starting with

---

Back at Work

When we were working on BoundsChecker 5 at NuMega, we knew our internals team was going to be ahead of our UI team. Yet we needed to make sure that we could test the product even if we wouldn't have a UI for a month or more. The internals team developed simple drivers that called the subsystem with the data it needed to operate. With these drivers in place, we were able to test the product and make sure it was rock solid long before the UI was ready. In addition to testing the product earlier, these drivers provided a stable and simple way to automate the testing of the subsystems over multiple releases.

touch testing. In this type of testing, all the windows and dialog boxes are invoked and dismissed to make sure the breadth of the UI is functional.

TEAMS, PROCESS, AND CULTURE

Do you have a history of building quality software? Are your processes efficient and effective, or are they usually a time drain and resource sink? Does quality factor into everyone's view of product development? To what depths are you willing to go for quality? Is it everyone's passion or always "someone else's job"?

These are very important questions. They can help to reveal how successful a group has been in delivering quality software. Sometimes people say that senior management isn't willing to make the commitment necessary to deliver quality products. On the other hand, perhaps they want to ship a quality product but don't believe the team has a system that is effective or efficient. They believe that more QA processes will just add more time and increase costs without improving the product. One of the goals of this book is to define a practical set of QA processes that will allow you to ship the best product possible in the shortest time frame possible. Once you have a system you know will work, you are far more likely to support it and commit to it.

Back at Work

At NuMega, the project manager set the tone for the importance of quality to everyone on the team. Our project manager installed and used the product on almost a daily basis, logged bugs, and discussed recently found issues with the team at meetings, at lunch, and in the hallway. This set the pace for the rest of the team, and everyone got on board. Everyone tested. Everyone evaluated. Bugs were bad things and fixing them was important. To back all this up, we even devoted portions of people's reviews to the quality of their code or the number of bugs they found. We let people know that quality wasn't going to be ignored until the end of a project or forgotten after the product shipped.

WHAT, WHEN, AND HOW TO TEST

An effective and efficient testing process is based on knowing which part of the product to test and when and how to test it. Although this might seem simple, if you have a short or time-pressured schedule and a bare-bones staff, you must not waste a moment focusing your attention too broadly or too narrowly. You need to focus on testing four key areas of the product:

◆ Installation procedure

◆ Features

◆ Feature integration

◆ Performance

The testing of these areas needs to occur constantly during the development cycle. To do this effectively, however, you need to know when and how to test each of these areas. More specifically, you need a set of well-defined processes and procedures that catch problems for each major activity in the development process. These processes and procedures include:

◆ *Check-in tests*   Tests software before coding changes are submitted.

◆ *Daily smoke tests*   Tests software after every build.

◆ *Feature completion testing*   Tests a feature as soon as it's completed.

◆ *Stabilization and integration testing*   Tests feature integration at predefined intervals.

◆ *Beta and release candidate testing*   Tests the product externally at predefined intervals.

The remainder of this section will focus on these five key testing activities.

CHECK-IN TESTING

Check-in tests are designed to let developers test critical features on a local build before the code is checked in. To be successful, check-in tests must have the following characteristics:

◆ be extremely portable between machines

◆ be very easy to set up, run, and interpret (be automated)

◆ perform a valuable set of tests for key features or subsystems of the product

Check-in tests really show their value when you have made changes to a critical or complex part of the system. If you run a check-in test and it fails on your local build, you can find the problem and fix it yourself. You have not disrupted the work of all the other developers who might have pulled the buggy source files after you checked them in. In addition, check-in tests prevent a critical bug from entering into the daily build and causing the smoke test to break.

DAILY SMOKE TESTING

In addition to the check-in tests, another way you can implement your "test as soon as possible" strategy is to use daily smoke tests. Just as you are building the product every single day, you should test it every day. The smoke tests are a core set of automated regression tests that verify that the product's key features work. They assure that you had a good build and that you had no significant regression in the previous 24 hours. As new key features are added to the project over time, the smoke tests are also improved and augmented.

Back at Work

NuMega's BoundsChecker is well known for finding memory leaks and memory overruns in C/C++ applications. The daily smoke tests for BoundsChecker included a sample application called BugBench, which was full of memory leaks, memory overwrites, and other nasty bugs. We used this sample program to produce the errors that BoundsChecker should have been able to catch. If BoundsChecker could not find all the errors and memory leaks in the sample program, then, by definition, we had a bad build. We liked to have a "smoke test report" available in the morning that detailed the testing results of the prior night's build. With this process in place, our project was almost always stable and usable, because our smoke tests found critical problems right away.

Note that our daily smoke tests were not concerned about the smaller features of the product, such as whether the print preview feature worked or whether pressing F1 would invoke Help in all dialog boxes. These could be easily verified by manual testing. We were focused on the core features of the product.

Like the daily build, smoke test information (provided in a summary report) is shared with the whole team so that it's clear to everyone whether the product has a problem or not. If there is a problem, the QA and dev leads should investigate, identify the problem's root quickly, and assign it to an engineer for resolution. Solving the problem should be the engineer's top priority.

FEATURE COMPLETION TESTING

As previously mentioned, your goal is to test each feature as soon as it is complete. A software engineer and a QA engineer should be assigned to each major feature, and together they are responsible for delivering it on time and with high quality. This arrangement will encourage the two to work together and share information, ideas, and ultimately, failure or success. You should have automated tests ready for each major feature, but you must always be ready to test the features manually if necessary. Your QA plan should describe all of the above information so that it is clear when and how each feature gets tested.

Key Features

The QA team's general effort is focused on key feature testing. Feature testing validates that a specific feature works as needed. Key features can be tested with automation or be tested manually, but the key is to test a feature as soon as a developer has completed it. The sooner you can test the feature, the sooner you can objectively assess your progress and, if problems surface, work towards their resolution.

It's important to note that the QA engineer will almost always find problems with a feature. There must be some time built into the schedule for fixing these problems during the product's development. The time can be built into the feature itself or into the closest stabilization period. I favor adding a little time to both. For example, a five-day task should have an additional day just for fixing bugs—a 20 percent overhead.

Installation

Unfortunately, the installation procedure is one of the most neglected portions of any product. People don't often think of the installation as a major feature, so they don't give it the attention it deserves. Ignore installation testing at your own peril—the installation procedure is one feature in your product that everyone will use. If there's a way to create a great first impression, it's with the installation procedure. And if there's a single way to annoy the most users, it's also with the installation procedure.

Assign a feature team to validate the installation procedure just as you would for any other major product feature. In this case, you should assign release engineers and QA engineers to the tasks of creating and validating the installation procedure. These tasks should be part of your QA plan and occur regularly throughout the development process. You must remember that the installation procedure is usually a complicated piece of software and needs to work flawlessly on a wide variety of configurations. As you might expect, automated installation testing can do wonders in this regard.

The following is a list of the basic installation procedure testing that needs to be performed for any product you plan to ship:

◆ *Operating systems* Test all the operating systems supported by your software.

◆ *Service packs* Test all the service packs of the operating systems supported by your software.

◆ *Clean installs* Test the installation of the product on a system with no prior versions of the software.

◆ *Dirty installs* Test the installation of the product on a system with prior versions of the software.

◆ *Product configuration* Test the installation procedure's support of different product configurations.

◆ *Installation feature set* Test the installation procedure's own feature set (online registration, forward button, back button, cancel button, and so on).

◆ *Uninstall testing* Test the procedure for uninstalling the product.

Although you want to provide a good installation procedure for your customers, you will find that the installation procedure plays a very important role in accelerating the QA effort. Because your QA team should be testing with the latest build of the software, you want to make sure they have a solid installation procedure to use. You don't want the team wasting their time manually setting up the registry, copying files, editing configurations, and so on. You want them focused on product testing—not on manual, error-prone installation procedures.

A solid and easy-to-use installation procedure will benefit everyone on the team, not just QA. Each member of the team should be able to install the product for his or her own needs. Your tech writers need to be able

---

Back at Work

Don't forget the de-installation procedure! At NuMega, our development and QA teams appreciated a functional de-installation procedure because it allowed them to get a clean system without having to spend time manually deleting registry entries and files in the system directory.

---

to install the product to write about its features, your engineers need to be able to install the product to track down bugs and evaluate performance problems, and your usability engineers need to be able to install the product to evaluate the user interface. You want your team to use the product and not wrestle with its setup.

STABILIZATION AND INTEGRATION TESTING

So far in the development cycle, testing has focused on specific features. But with stabilization and integration testing, the focus is on the following:

- Completing any feature testing that might have been delayed.

- Testing feature integration.

- Testing current performance and load.

- Correcting or resolving all serious bugs, design flaws, or architectural issues.

- Testing beta releases and release candidates.

Completing each one of these steps is very important to the next leg of the project. Let's take a look at each one of them in more detail.

Completion of Feature Testing

Your first priority is to finalize any testing that might have been delayed. It is quite common for at least one feature team to need more time to complete their testing effort, even after four to six weeks of heavy-duty activity. Use this time to perform any testing that has not yet been completed so you can keep your teams testing in parallel for the rest of the project.

Integration Testing

Integration testing should be defined ahead of time as part of the test plan. The best way to do this is to have a set of scenarios, preferably from the user's point of view, describing how the different features should work together. Before testing begins, you should be able to state with confidence that a certain set of the features are operational and will work together. This is the time to test them—and if they don't work, this is the time to fix them.

Performance and Load Testing

Although it's true that the final product can't be truly evaluated until the entire system has been assembled, it's also true that observations and preliminary measurements can be taken to evaluate the progress—or lack of it—during the course of development.

Be sure to create a set of tests that will serve as your performance or load benchmarks for the product, and carry out these tests regularly during the course of development. Do stress tests, and evaluate the performance of the system at key milestones and during synchronization and integration periods. That's what these periods are for. Doing tests during these periods is your best chance to catch problems early and fix them before you start building on top of your mistake.

Back at Work

Performance was an important issue with the development of BoundsChecker. It was easy to add a few lines of code to a critical feature and completely change the performance characteristics of the product. To address this problem, we had several test applications that would stress BoundsChecker to its limits. One such test application was called Torture. It created 256 concurrent threads and allocated and freed tens of thousands of small blocks off the heap. Throughout the course of development, we ran the Torture program (and others like it) to see if the product's performance or load had degraded. Because we wanted this immediate feedback, we learned to run Torture as part of our automated regression tests every night and to compare the run-time performance. With this level of checking, we could usually track performance degradations to a change in the previous day's build. Quite nice!

Correction After Testing

The stabilization and integration period is also an opportunity for the team to fix important bugs before moving on to the next set of features. Testing the features and their integration will result in a lot of bugs—and that is exactly what you want. You can then weed out these bugs early so that future efforts will be more productive. But you must plan time to fix and address these issues.

Assessment and Evaluation After Testing

When the stabilization and integration period is coming to a close, be sure to assess the results and make changes as needed. Need more hardware? Need to test a subsystem better? Need better definition of APIs? Need more people? Whatever changes are necessary should be made immediately.

This is also the best time to anticipate what can be improved upon for the next stabilization and integration period. Look at the stabilization and integration phase as a test of the team as well as the software—you should evaluate the progress and performance of both and make whatever changes might be required.

An Example of Testing

Let's look at a very simple example to see how all these areas play together. Suppose you're building a Web application, and you are at the stabilization and integration phase. You expect to have certain functionality available; for example, maybe all you can do is create, modify and delete customers. However, these capabilities represent a good chunk of work. They indicate that the UI, Web server, middleware, and database backend are tied together. Under these circumstances, your integration testing might consist of the following:

- Attempt to create a customer.
- Attempt to create an invalid customer (field validation).
- Attempt to create a duplicate customer.
- Attempt to modify an existing customer (all fields, no fields).
- Attempt to modify a nonexistent customer.
- Attempt to incorrectly modify an existing customer.
- Attempt to delete an existing customer.
- Attempt to delete an invalid customer.

After you have finished this integration testing, you will have some measurements of the application's performance. How long does it take to create a customer? To delete a customer? To have an error returned? Although there might be many reasons for poor performance, if you can't create a new customer quickly with a small database, you might have a problem that needs to be reviewed. Is there a problem with the database drivers? Do you have a poor database design? A poor middleware design? To make sure you are monitoring performance over time, set up a baseline or target for your basic transactions and compare performance regularly so you know if you are staying on target or if you are diverging from it.

The point of integration testing is to make sure that the product is functionally sound at this first checkpoint. If it is, you're ready to move on to the next major milestone. If it isn't—for example, if you can't create, modify, and delete customers—then you should stop and fix whatever is preventing you from moving on.

BETA AND RELEASE CANDIDATE TESTING

Beta testing and release candidate testing are key milestones in your project. A beta test is an opportunity to have customers test and evaluate your software months before it is manufactured or used in production environments. Most projects have one to three beta periods in the second half of their development effort. Each beta involves dozens to hundreds and sometimes even thousands of users. A release candidate—potentially the final build of the product—is even more important. It represents the software that you intend to release to customers if your last round of testing is completed without serious problems. (See Chapter 13 for a complete discussion of beta testing and Chapter 14 for release candidates.)

One of the challenges of working with beta and release candidates is deciding what needs to be tested on the build before it is released externally. Surely you won't be able to retest the product completely—after all, it took you months, if not years, to test the product and get it to this state. Instead, you need to have a very specific and well-defined test plan that can be executed in a very short amount of time. (Seven to ten days is normal for most small to mid-sized projects.) Beta and release candidate testing should involve the following tasks:

- Executing the fully automated test suite
- Executing a predefined set of manual tests, including:
    - Sanity installation / license testing (all that are not automated)
    - Core product feature testing (all that are not automated)

- Critical performance and load testing (all that are not automated)
- Spot testing on all supported platforms
- Other areas of specific concern to the project

While this list is a good start, you must detail specific testing scenarios for each of the topics above. If you can successfully execute all of your tests, then you can release your software. If you can't execute them all successfully, you need to fix the problem and repeat the process.

One of the characteristics of a good beta and release candidate testing cycle is that it's predictable. You should know how long your automated tests run, and you should know how long it takes to execute your manual testing process. Given this information, you should be able to accurately predict the time required to test another beta or release candidate, should that be required. Knowing how long it will take to cycle through another build and how well you can test it can help you decide how risky and costly any additional change could be.

Who Should Test?

Everyone who is involved with the project should be responsible for testing it. It doesn't matter who the person is and what their role is. When anyone uses the product for any reason and in any form, they must do so with a critical eye. Whether you're the project manager gleefully looking at a new feature, a user education writer reviewing how certain tasks work together, or a human factors engineer installing the product to check out the user interface, you must look for, find, and report quality problems.

Again, in time-pressured, resource-short environments, you can't assume that one group of people will be able to do the whole testing job, especially since the QA team is often the most understaffed. So be sure to have your developers, technical writers, human factors engineer, product manager, project manager, vice president, or summer intern look for problems every time they use the product for their own needs. And at all costs, have them report problems when they find them.

When it comes to stabilization and integration periods, the entire development team tests—it's a team effort. It's a chance for the team to see where it is and how much more it needs to do. The QA lead traditionally drives this effort by assigning testing responsibilities to each member of the project team. Most of the time, these assignments focus on areas where the team's automated test beds are the weakest. The assignments also ask members to execute manual testing plans or to "play user" on key parts of the product. The bottom line: There's just no substitute for the whole development team pounding on the product over the course of the development cycle. It's something that you need to make part of your culture and one of your most basic processes.

To take this concept further, another valuable technique is to use your software internally. This concept, called *eating your own dog food*, is well known in the industry and can prove to be extremely valuable. There's nothing like using software for real work to help get quality problems identified and resolved. Even if you can't use your product within your own development team, try having some sophisticated users experiment with it. You might be surprised at what they discover.

At some point, it becomes important to clearly distinguish the testing responsibilities of the team members (particularly developers) from the QA team's testing responsibilities. It's important to have a clear division of labor so that people can concentrate on their respective responsibilities.

The developers are critical to the quality of the product. After all, they are closest to the code and are in the best position to create or eliminate problems. To make sure that bugs are caught before the QA team even sees a feature,

---

Back at Work

At NuMega, we were trying to get the beta 2 release of BoundsChecker version 3 ready. We had daily meetings to review progress. Carol, our QA lead (she was the entire QA team at the time), retorted emphatically that the build was utterly worthless. She said she wasn't wasting any more of her time testing it, was going home until the developers got their acts together, and promptly left.

I could have stood up and cheered. Although I wasn't pleased at all with the state of the beta, Carol let the developers know that they were responsible for the basic testing of the software and for working out code problems themselves. With the quality so far below the line, she had to call a time-out and point out the problem. The development team got the message. We agreed to have everyone test and fix the software until we felt we were ready to have Carol come back. It took about two days.

they must work at testing their software as it's written. A good developer can accelerate the effort of the QA team by giving the team solid features to work with. Conversely, a poor developer can slow down the effort of the QA team by delivering features with problems large enough that they prevent any significant testing. There's nothing more frustrating to a QA engineer than to find lots of obvious problems that could have been found by a developer with just a few minutes of work.

In regards to testing, the developers have certain responsibilities:

- Review of the test plan

- Unit level testing (Does a feature work for most common situations?)

- Preliminary system integration testing (Does a feature work with other features?)

- The logging or fixing of every bug that they find in their own use of the software

The QA team builds off this basic work. They trust that the level of testing just listed has been completed before the development team delivers the feature. They aren't blissfully wishing that all is well; they are simply assuming that there will be a sufficient level of quality to allow them to do their job. If this isn't the case, it will become apparent to everyone very quickly.

The QA team now takes the feature testing to the next level. They focus on the following:

- Test planning

- Automation development

- Automation execution

- Feature permutation testing

- Installation testing

- Integration and systems testing

- Performance and load testing

- Manual testing (for features that are not automated)

- Problem diagnosis and problem reporting

- Verification of fixes and closure of bugs

Although all of the responsibilities listed above should be familiar to the QA team, the last one might be less so. Only the QA engineer on the feature team should close a bug. The developer's job is to fix the bug in the code, check it into the source code management system, and update the status of the bug to "Fixed" in the bug tracking system. But it is the QA engineer's responsibility to review all fixed bugs and make sure they are indeed taken care of. Once this verification occurs, the bug can be officially closed.

OTHER CRITICAL QA TOPICS

There are a few additional topics that almost every team will need to address. These include the problem of testing on a wide range of platforms, the proper role and use of manual testing, and the need to have a sufficient testing infrastructure for the project's needs. Let's take a look at each one.

CONFIGURATION TESTING MATRIX

One of the most time-consuming tasks of the QA function is the testing of the product on a wide range of software configurations. Most products today support multiple operating systems and need to work on a wide variety of configurations. Testing the product on all these configurations, if it were done manually, would be a mammoth undertaking.

Fortunately, you have a way of minimizing this task significantly. If you have solid automated tests beds that focus on the most important features of the product, you can use these on all the configurations you choose to support.

Back at Work

We approached the configuration-testing problem at NuMega by assigning specific configurations to developers and testers. One person got Microsoft Windows 95, another got Microsoft Windows 98, another Microsoft Windows NT 3.51, and yet another Microsoft Windows NT 4.0. Each person was required to test on his or her assigned configuration in the hope of finding problems early in the development process. With this simple approach, we got decent coverage and found showstopper problems almost immediately.

Manual Testing

With all the emphasis I've put on automated testing, some of you might be wondering if there is a value to manual testing. Yes, there is, but you have to know when to apply it. Use manual testing under the following circumstances:

- *For key features when automation is late or nonexistent* What if you don't have the time or resources to get all the automated testing written, and the development team has just delivered a feature? In this event, you've got to do manual testing just to make sure the feature is evaluated in a timely manner. Finding and fixing bugs early is the overriding goal.

- *For nonvolatile, low-risk features* There are times when the value of automation loses to the simplicity and timeliness of manual testing. If a minor feature is easy to test and not likely to change, it makes sense to skip the automation effort in deference to more important tasks.

- *When crunches hit* When time crunches hit and you need to do a lot of testing in a short amount of time, many people like to add more testers—often people with little or no background in the product. To do this effectively, you need a solid manual test plan. The plan should discuss the most important product areas to test and which areas need to be verified. Optimize the plan for breadth rather than depth, and then encourage testers to dig into their assigned areas. This approach will allow you to assign coverage areas easily and know that you've got the critical parts of the product covered.

Just remember: Don't become dependent on manual testing. It is very costly to scale, and it makes testing in parallel with product development more difficult.

Equipment for Testing

In time-pressured projects, you must make sure the team is not slowed down due to a lack of basic hardware or software. Although equipment needs will vary greatly among teams and projects, the following is a list of some of the basic needs you should meet:

- *Two to three computers for each QA engineer*   One computer can be used for production: e-mail, bug reports, automation development, and so on. The other computers should be used for in-office testing. The testing computers should be ghosted so they can be easily rebuilt at almost any time. It's also a good idea if one of these machines is representative of an end-user's machine.

- *Two computers for each developer*   Remember, developers test too. They need one computer for their development environment and another for testing. Developers can configure the second computer as needed for bug hunting and can remain productive if serious configuration or software problems require a rebuild. Again, it's a good idea if one of the machines is representative of an end-user's machine.

- *An online software library*   All software that is needed for development or testing should be available online. A CD library or jukebox

---

Back at Work

In the early days of NuMega, we didn't have an online software library and the hunt for CDs was frustrating and wasted valuable time. Often our product plans required us to support the latest operating system or compilers from Microsoft. Fortunately, we were a beta site and received regular updates. Unfortunately, we got only one CD. When someone needed the last beta of Windows or Visual Studio, the hunt for the CD began!

If we were lucky, we would find the person who had the CDs we were looking for, but most of the time we would follow the "I gave it to X" trail. (I followed one of these trails five levels deep one day, only to have the last person in the chain deny that he ever had it!) If that didn't work, we would send an e-mail message—and then wait for a reply while we hopefully had something else productive to do.

After seeing several dozen messages like this over a couple of months, we finally realized we had to solve this problem, especially as we grew larger. The online CD library was our solution. It worked, but only when we put it online. Our attempt at a physical library system failed because people who borrowed the CDs never returned them and we ended up back where we started—who's got the CD?

is a great way to make sure the team has quick and easy access to the tools, products, and operating systems it needs to perform its work. Naturally, you'll need to make sure you have proper licensing, but it's well worth the price if you don't want your QA team walking the halls looking for CDs.

◆   *A test lab*   A test lab is a great asset. Having a rack of testing computers set up with a variety of operating systems, language editions, and service packs can greatly simplify the QA effort for the entire team. In addition, a test lab is also great for setting up complicated test environments that require a lot of time to build and configure.

These recommendations will certainly increase the hardware and software budget, but the added costs are quite insignificant when compared to the productivity and quality improvements that they will produce.

COMMON PROBLEMS AND SOLUTIONS

The following are some of the typical problems and questions that surface when applying these techniques, and some solutions to these problems.

LACK OF RESOURCES

Lack of resources (and in this case, I mean people resources) is probably the most common problem with QA and is, frankly, more complex than it might appear. If you don't have the QA resources you need, first figure out the nature of the problem. If you are always short of QA resources but have open positions, you might have a recruiting problem, and you should revisit the discussion in Chapter 1. If your QA staff crunch is a result of a spike of extra work or a shortened deadline, you might want to consider hiring temporary contractors. Before moving in this direction, however, you must have your QA test plans in place. It's very important that the contractors *execute* your QA plan—not write it.

However, if you simply have more QA work than your staff can handle, then you have only two choices if you want to ship a quality product:

◆   Redefine the schedule to meet the feature and staffing constraints.

◆   Redefine the features to meet the schedule and staffing constraints.

With the first option, you need to spread the QA work among the existing team members. This will usually push the schedule out further because they are required to take on additional work. However, you know that you are holding the line on quality while at the same time keeping the staffing, features, and schedule balanced. Before choosing this option, you must consider the morale of the team, the current length of and your position in the development cycle, and the impact of a delay in entering the market.

With the second option, you keep the schedule (which is often critical) and maintain the quality of the product (just as critical). The reason this option works so well is that it lessens the overall load on the *entire* team and reduces overall project risk. Because you don't need to develop, test, or document the features you eliminate, you get the product out quicker. Before choosing this option, you should carefully consider the features and how important they are to your success. I've found that it's more important to ship early with a few great features than to ship later with the extras. (In Chapter 11, I discuss prioritizing your feature set for situations like this.)

LACK OF PREPARATION

Many projects start off on the wrong foot and, frankly, are doomed from the very beginning because team members simply don't prepare ahead of time for the effort that is needed. You need to have the basic plans, automation, and equipment described earlier. In addition, you need to have almost all of these at the start of development. If you're writing plans or waiting for equipment to arrive during the development cycle, you're already behind and are not doing what you should be doing—testing!

As the full scope of the QA effort becomes clear, teams often consider adding resources to the project. Whether these resources are contract employees or internal transfers, it's unlikely that they'll have any specific knowledge of the product itself. They won't be able to run any automated tests (possibly because there aren't any), or they won't be able to execute manual tests because there are no checklists or overview material about what needs to be done. In this case, the best way to move forward is to have them play "user." Although this approach often produces valuable ad-hoc testing, it shouldn't be confused with or be a replacement for the type of testing I have discussed in this chapter.

Lack of Automation

I hope it is clear by now how valuable automated testing is to the QA effort. Without automation, your manual testing effort and labor needs will skyrocket, and testing will significantly delay your schedule. It is critical that the QA (and development) teams write as much automation as possible—and certainly not less than the automation guidelines I previously described.

Lack of Execution or Commitment

When a project is suffering from quality problems, it's not always a result of ignorance of QA concepts or techniques. Instead, it's often a lack of execution or commitment. If you were to interview the managers or leads of such a project about QA, they would probably do a great job describing what should be done. But when you look at their projects, it's just not happening. In terms of focus, concern, and commitment, putting quality into a product takes effort. It is not simply a theoretical argument, but an active and passionate activity that needs to be carried out by all team members.

Lack of Appropriate Focus

I strongly encourage teams to test the breadth of their product before testing the depth. Make sure all the major features that are completed are in good working order before spending time on the minor features. Of course, you need to have these features prioritized, as I mentioned earlier. All too often, however, teams spend way too much time on a narrow feature area while the rest of the product is falling apart. Think of the construction of a building. There's no real value in polishing the chrome in the lobby when the elevators don't work.

7

Release Engineering Fundamentals

Building and installing software has become an increasingly difficult task. In fact, it's now so complicated that a specialized discipline
called release engineering is devoted to it. The release engineering function
is critical to shipping on time. In this chapter, I'll discuss the fundamentals
of release engineering and how this function makes it possible for us to do
our day-to-day work.

Whether your organization is large or small, you must be able to build
and install your software product on a regular basis. Too often, however,
development teams can't build or install their own software for weeks or
even months. Even worse, no one has final responsibility for build and
installation issues, so the problem lingers over the course of development.
Because the project can't be built or installed, all sorts of problems can creep
in and cause delays. If you can't be certain about the actual state of your
software because you can't see it or use it, you are flying blind. To apply the
concepts described in this book, you must be able to build and install the software at will.

RELEASE ENGINEERS

Release engineers are project team members who are skilled in the processes
and technology of building and installing software. Although release engineers can have a wide variety of responsibilities, the most important ones for
the purpose of this discussion are the following:

- Define, create, and maintain the product's build environment.
- Define, create, and maintain the product's installation procedure.
- Define, create, and maintain patch kits or service packs.
- Conduct unit testing and basic quality assurance of the installa-
  tion procedure.
- Develop tools, scripts, and automation for the release engineer-
  ing processes.
- Plan for the build environment (the build lab).

To accomplish these tasks, release engineers must be an integral part of
the software project team from beginning to end. They should create a build
and installation plan based on the project requirements as they are currently understood. They should be part of project status meetings and have
build and installation deliverables just like any other members of the team.

Back at Work

At NuMega, we didn't have dedicated release engineers, but we did have a team that performed a release engineering function. Our team initially consisted of a support engineer and a human factors engineer. Despite what you might think, they made a great part-time release engineering team, and they did a solid job for over a year. Remember: Talented people can take on many tasks. But one day, they phoned me from the build lab (actually, a cubicle) where they were wrestling with ever more complicated build and installation scripts. Their message was clear: "Ed, we've had it. Hire a release engineer!"

In the smallest groups, there might be no need for full-time, dedicated release engineers. Instead, these responsibilities might be assigned to other team members as a part-time job. But over time, as the complexity of the software increases and the size of the development team grows, dedicated release engineers will become necessary. And over still more time, a central release engineering organization will be required. Just because this function might not be a full-time job at the beginning, don't assume that it is not important or that the quality of its work doesn't matter.

BUILDS

A build is a compilation of all the product source code. To build your software correctly, you must have the most basic level of integration possible—source code integration. Your source code integrity must be perfect; you can't have any complication or linkage errors. In large, complex projects, this perfection is particularly difficult because of the many interrelationships between the source code modules. However, it is both possible and important to build your software regularly.

WHY THEY'RE IMPORTANT

As I said earlier, the ability to build the software is fundamental to your ability to ship software on time. Building regularly forces integration. One

Back at Work

When I first arrived at NuMega, one of our most talented engineers (Matt Pietrek) was the only person who could build the entire product. Even though the team and the product were still small, the build environment was incredibly complex. Matt was literally the only engineer who knew what to do. To build the product, he would go into his office and close the door. Like a mad scientist, he would juggle three different compilers and half a dozen scripts. He would manually edit configuration files, build files, linker files, and option files. Then after three or four hours of intense work, he'd wave a magic wand and we'd usually have a build—assuming he hadn't found any problems.

Although the news of success was wonderful, losing our top engineer for a half-day just to complete a build prevented us from running a parallel software development model. Changing this situation quickly became a priority.

of the most common problems in software engineering is getting all the pieces to work together. If left until the end, this job often requires weeks or months of work. In the worst cases, it can require redefinition of APIs and components. And this, of course, means delays—most of which were never planned for.

With regular builds, software engineers can be assured that the code integrates. The APIs, header files, parameters, data types, and macros must all be consistent, or the software won't build correctly. A build failure forces developers to communicate and, if necessary, change the software. But this process is exactly what you want—to find and fix integration problems early rather than late, such as the day before you're supposed to code freeze for beta.

How to Do Them

The following are some recommendations on how to make the build task easier and more effective.

The Make Utility

The Make utility maintains a set of build rules and relationships for the software—either for the application or for a component. By describing these build rules, the Make utility can decide which images need to be built and which source files need to be compiled or linked.

The Make utility has been around for decades, starting first on UNIX and then being adopted on virtually all other development platforms. It is one of the most essential tools for building software. It has been improved over the years, and the latest version, called Nmake, is available with Microsoft Visual Studio. Be sure to investigate the Make utility for your development environment, and be sure to use it to automate the tasks required to build your software.

Build Numbers

Developers use build numbers to uniquely identify builds. The build number is a monotonically increasing integer that is never repeated for the history of an application. It continues to increase through base levels, milestones, and even software releases.

When you can build your application easily, the chances are pretty good that there will be many different builds in your development and testing environments. Over time, being able to identify the specific build that is installed on a machine, as well as the software components that accompany it, becomes very important. So does identifying the build in which key bugs were fixed or introduced. After the software is released to customers, the ability to identify specific builds will be even more critical.

The build number is increased each time a build is done. The build procedure usually increases the number at the start of the build operation and then places it in a resource file so that all components can include it or link against it. The build number is typically added to the About command on the application's Help menu so that users can see which build they are using.

Build Machines and Labs

The build environment is the set of software applications, tools, libraries, and compilers that are needed to compile and link the software. It's often best to stage this environment on a set of dedicated build machines that are owned and operated exclusively by the release engineering team and that are not subject to change. It's also important that you back these machines up regularly and make sure they can be restored quickly and easily. And don't forget to install virus-checking software on the build machines to prevent unexpected complications.

As the number of build machines grows, you might need a build lab. A lab is very useful when you need to build really large applications in parallel, or when you have many products to build at the same time (perhaps nightly). A build lab also helps secure the build machines and prevent accidental tampering.

Notification and Failure

When a build is done, the project team needs to be notified. You could send the build notification to the project team's distribution list, or you might want to set up a specialized build distribution list.

Notifying everyone is especially important if a build fails. When failure occurs, it's critical that the dev lead or some equally qualified person look at the error log and determine the nature of the problem. This person owns the problem until it has been assigned to a specific engineer for resolution, and fixing the build problem must then become his or her top priority.

Evaluation and Management

After the build is complete, it should be sent to a network share where it can be evaluated by the automated tests created by the QA team. The evaluation is an important step because a complete build doesn't tell you whether you actually have a usable product—you only know that you can compile and link all the files.

One of the best ways to evaluate the build is to install the product and run the automated smoke tests mentioned in Chapter 6. To manage this process effectively, you should have two target directories for the builds:

◆ *Most Recent Build (MRB)* This directory contains the most recent build of the software. The build might or might not install or work correctly, however.

◆ *Last Known Good Build (LKGB)* This directory contains the last known good build. When you are certain that the current build is good—it installs and passes smoke tests—copy the contents of the MRB directory to the LKGB directory.

The team should install from the LKGB directory for their day-to-day work. In most instances, the QA team moves the most recent build into LKGB as soon as it has been evaluated. If there is a problem with the most recent build, the team can still function because the build in the LKGB is still functional.

Accountability, Penalties, and Metrics

As I discussed in Chapter 4, at NuMega we decided not to have a lot of processes. But we were very serious about the processes that we did have, and we followed them. Building the product was one of those critical processes. We decided that if someone broke a build, the build-breaker would buy donuts or bagels the next morning for the entire team. This simple but effective strategy emphasized the need to maintain the build and associated some sort of penalty with breaking it. For those teams that didn't have a release engineer, the penalty for breaking the build was that the build-breaker assumed the release engineering tasks until the next build break occurred.

Another way to emphasize the importance of the build process is to measure it. Monitor how many times the build breaks over time and perhaps who is contributing the most to breakage. Knowing that the build process is monitored can encourage individuals to be more disciplined with check-ins. You can also monitor how long the team can go without breaking the build and offer incentives for achievement in this area. In a large organization, you might even consider arranging a competition with other teams.

Check-In Frequency and Build Verification

Given the emphasis on not breaking the build, two of the most common questions are:

◆ *When do I have to check in my code?* Check in your code when you have some value to add to the project. The value might be as simple as a set of API stubs or as complicated as an update to a major feature, but you should try to check in your code frequently. The idea is to get everybody's code working together as early as possible.

◆ *How can I be sure I won't break the build?* If possible, build the software locally before checking in your code. You should be pulling source code from the source code management system on a regular basis, integrating your code, and checking it back in. For most projects, this process is fairly simple and is a great way to make sure you didn't break the build. As an additional incentive, you can run check-in tests (described in Chapter 6) to make sure there have been no feature regressions.

INSTALLATION PROCEDURE

The installation procedure software is critical—not just for the customer but for the development team as well. Unfortunately, the installation procedure is often the last portion of the project that is built, and the project can suffer because of it. In this section, I'll discuss why the installation procedure is so important and how you can build your installation procedure in parallel with the product's development effort.

WHY IT'S IMPORTANT

The installation procedure serves two important functions. First, the installation procedure forces the team to think about the setup environment the product will need. The installation procedure also requires that you know the application's bill of materials—the images, libraries, components, help files, type libraries, read me files, and so on that comprise the application. The procedure also forces you to define the run-time environment, including database drivers, common components, and operating systems support. If you can keep the product's contents valid and up to date, you will prevent major problems down the road.

Second, with an installation procedure in place, team members have easy access to the most recent builds of the software. They don't have to know all the messy details associated with setting it up, such as the location of files, component registration procedures, startup commands, registry settings, and so on. Team members can simply install the product and use it for their needs, as follows:

◆ Software engineers can see how their features work from the official build and can evaluate bugs or problems using the same installation procedure that the rest of the team is using.

◆ The QA team can install and test the software for problems on a regular basis. Not only will their automated regression tests be run on the latest builds, but all testing by the entire team will be done using the last known good build. This practice assures that you are testing against the most recent, most stable software. In addition, a single official build makes it much easier to decide whether features are working. The fact that a developer can get a feature to work on his or her machine doesn't matter if the feature doesn't work in the official build. If it doesn't work in the official build, as installed by the current installation procedure, the feature doesn't work.

◆ Technical writers need to see, use, and evaluate the software to document it correctly. Access to an installable build of the product greatly accelerates their work because new features dropped into the build by developers can be seen and documented the next day by the technical writers.

◆ As the builds chug along, human factors engineers can watch the product's user interface come alive and provide evaluation, insight, and advice. Without official builds, the human factors engineers simply do not have ease of access to the features they need to perform their work on a timely basis. As a result, they will find design flaws and inconsistencies too late in the development process.

◆ The project manager's ability to manage the project is also greatly enhanced. The official build provides excellent visibility into the current state of the project. There's no secrecy about the status of features, performance, quality, online help, and so on.

◆ Finally, having an installation procedure available early extends the feedback circle to other groups such as product management, technical support, and sales. Each of these groups can provide valuable feedback about the progress of the product, and they might catch a few bugs, too.

How to Do It

Although exact implementation details vary widely across different products and applications, the approach to the installation procedure is always the same. You start building the installation procedure at the very beginning of the project, and then you add to it over time.

The Skeleton

The first step in building an installation procedure is to construct the skeleton. The goal is simple: Get the first set of files copied to their target directories. Even if the program can do nothing more than display "Hello World," you should build an installation procedure for it. It doesn't have to be complicated, but you should at least create an infrastructure you can build on.

The Flesh

Next you want to build on the basic structure you have created, adding more complexity and sophistication as the project progresses. The idea is to advance the installation procedure in parallel with the project's development, so you build the skeleton first and grow it over time. For example, as new software features are completed, new operating systems or databases are supported, or new license requirements are clarified, you should add their files and support requirements.

I'm not suggesting this effort be ad hoc, however—that would only produce a mess. What I am suggesting is that you add features to the installation procedure as necessary. Your goal is to write an installation procedure development plan that provides specific features and support for the development and testing teams as they need it. This plan should help you guard against the two extremes of either making changes every day or not meeting the needs of the team in a timely manner.

The Kit

The kit is the set of files that are shipped to the user. The kit-building process (kitting) binds the installation procedure with the files it needs to install. As a result, the files are often compressed and are not always representative of what is actually placed on the user's system. It's wise to define what goes into the kitting process and what comes out. It's also a great idea to design a test that assures the presence of the correct number of files with approximately the correct sizes and dates. For this purpose, an automated, table-driven application to verify kit contents can be very useful.

PULLING IT ALL TOGETHER

Once you have the basics of builds and installations in place, you need to pull the whole thing together into an automated, factory-like process. It's critical that this process be set up at the beginning of the project—perhaps it should be the first task.

The following is a list of the fundamental steps of a build cycle:

◆ Build the images.

◆ Create the kit.

◆ Test the kit.

◆ Send a build pass or fail message.

◆ Run smoke tests to validate the build.

◆ If successful, copy the build to the LKGB directory.

◆ Send a smoke test pass or fail message.

DAILY BUILDS, DAILY KITS, AND DAILY TESTS

The daily process of building, kitting, and testing is the heartbeat of a project. You should run this process every night and review the results in the morning in order to understand the exact state of the project. With this process, you can make informed, intelligent decisions about what needs to be changed. Without this process, you are flying blind and will never know whether the project is coming together—or even if it can come together—until it's too late to do anything about it. Then all you can do is slip the schedule.

THE SELL

In organizations that have already adopted these concepts, people already know that builds, installs, and smoke tests can be done on a daily basis. But in other organizations, people might be skeptical. They are typically too busy, have no resources, and are struggling to get other work done. Who's got time

> ### *Back at Work*
>
> In the early days, the concept of a daily build was very new to our company. We were a small engineering team and starting a daily build process was very difficult. There wasn't a lot of support for it and it was difficult getting the build environment, build machines, and processes set up.
>
> One day, I asked whether the daily build was successful. The engineer's response was "You mean we have to do this build thing EVERY day?" Yes, the daily build needed to be done every day. It was part of our development model, and it was critical to the way we worked.
>
> Years later, it's fun to look back on those days. The daily build is part of our culture now, and there is zero resistance to it. It's largely taken for granted, and when a build fails, there's a general outcry from everyone.

for this stuff? I've been there and I know it can be really hard. But the benefits are huge if you can make it happen. My recommendation is to sell the team on the ideas and then take it step by step—first get the builds working, then the installs, and finally the smoke tests.

COMMON PROBLEMS AND SOLUTIONS

The following are some of the typical problems and questions that surface when applying these techniques, and some solutions to those problems.

NO RELEASE ENGINEER

Be sure to factor release engineering activities into your project plans and schedule. Some teams don't recognize the significant amount of work that the release engineering effort requires. As a result, they are often caught by surprise and need to add time to the end of the schedule. Worse still is for this role never to be officially recognized, and for the build and installation procedure never to be fully owned and maintained.

LACK OF AUTOMATION

Automating the building, kitting, and testing processes is critical. Performing these tasks by hand will consume a lot of time and effort that could be better spent elsewhere.

A Late Installation Procedure

Some teams build the binaries frequently but don't perform the installation procedure until the end of the project. This approach can lower project visibility, and the ease of access benefits that come from early installation are lost to all the team members. In addition, team members often discover that the installation procedure takes far longer and is more complex than they originally thought it would be, and that it too needs some time to be shaken out. Unfortunately, developing anything late, including the installation procedure, adds risk and has the potential to push the schedule out.

Discipline

The daily building, kitting, and testing processes will break down. If the team does not have the discipline to attend to the issues, or if they start leaving problems unaddressed, you will not realize any of the benefits discussed previously. The team must have a culture of fixing problems. Everyone on the team must have the discipline to face these issues as they arise.

II

PROJECT DEFINITION AND PLANNING

8

Requirements

T his chapter covers the structure of the software requirements process. If your project is to have any chance of success, everyone on your team should have a solid understanding of what you want to build, why you want to build it, and what its most important features are. This understanding is best achieved through a well-defined and strictly controlled set of requirements. But it's also important to allow for iteration and improvement of the software. You want to be able to improve the product incrementally—even to the point of adding new features and removing others. These two needs—strict control and freedom to evolve—often seem poised against each other. Let's look at each one.

The first approach requires a specific, detailed, and rigid set of requirements that articulates almost every detail of the product. These requirements are complemented with a strict set of processes for managing change. The problem with this method is that it's hard to develop a detailed list of requirements, especially when you're working in new and innovative areas. This method also does not easily support incremental improvement or feedback. Even if it were possible to create a detailed set of requirements, it would often be ambiguous in written form and very difficult to keep current.

The second approach argues that a simple, general list of requirements is all that's needed. The idea here is to allow the team the freedom to make major feature implementation decisions during development; a more dynamic environment will enable the team to adapt and respond to new ideas and market demands. The problem with this approach is that it's filled with risk and uncertainty. It would be difficult to create a schedule and even more difficult to manage workflow. Testing and documentation would suffer because there would be insufficient information about the product to start working until late in the release when the true functionality of the product has emerged.

Which camp is right? Certainly both have advantages that are important and necessary to your project. You need a way to establish the fundamental requirements up front, before coding starts, and you need to allow controlled changes during the development cycle. In this chapter, we'll discuss a requirements management process that can help you strike the balance you need.

ESTABLISHING A COMMON VISION

At the beginning of each release you must establish a simple and clear vision statement. This statement should make your team's goals and priorities explicit; it is critical to uniting their efforts and assuring that they are working together.

A good vision statement has one overall theme that the entire team, if not the entire company, can rally around. The vision statement should not just drive the development effort but should also be instrumental in the positioning, marketing, and rollout of the product. The vision statement should unite all the groups involved in the commercial success of the product.

Although large projects might have multiple themes, you still need to keep the focus tight. Vision statements need to be short and clear; they should offer a challenge to excellence in one or two specific areas. The vision statement is usually the result of extensive, careful market and business analysis. It's not chosen lightly. You need to make sure your vision statement will provide significant commercial reward when it's achieved.

At NuMega, we always tried to create excitement about our releases by stating that we wanted to be quickest to market or first to use a new technology. In some projects we even dedicated a release to winning industry awards. The following are some of the vision statements that served to unite our product efforts in the past:

- ◆ Prevent new competitors from entering the marketing by delivering the most comprehensive error detection product for C/C++ programmers.

- ◆ Deliver the industry's easiest-to-use performance analysis product and get external recognition for its simplicity.

- ◆ Deliver the most powerful and sophisticated kernel debugger for Windows NT that the world has ever seen.

These statements were instrumental in guiding our feature selection and implementation processes. They also played a critical role in making tradeoffs. For example, if a choice had to be made between two conflicting needs, looking to the theme made it clear which one should be selected.

FINDING AND SOLVING USER PROBLEMS

After you have the vision statement in place, it's time to focus on the user's needs. At this point in the requirements definition process, you should be concerned about the problems the user would like solved rather than the specific tasks the user would like to perform. Let's take an example from one of the vision statements on the previous page. If you want to provide the most thorough error detection product for C/C++ programmers, you have to learn what the most common and most difficult programming errors are. Let's take another example. If you want to provide the easiest–to-use performance analysis product, you must understand what performance information is critical to users and how they want to see this information.

To support your understanding of the user's problems, it's important to solicit customer feedback and test your assumptions. The best way to confirm your plans or to work through internal debates is to get credible external feedback.

Back at Work

In our BoundsChecker 3.0 release, there was a lot of debate about the feature set of the product. We would discuss and even argue about these topics for weeks without any real progress. After a while, people wanted to ignore the topic altogether just to avoid an argument. To break this gridlock and restore morale, we decided to invite a group of customers and potential users to a pizza party, complete with giveaways. At the party, we demonstrated different feature ideas and asked them for input. Getting external data—and having the development team present to hear it—made it much easier to develop a compromise and define a solution that had a good chance of success.

DEFINING THE REQUIREMENTS

Once you have defined the vision and understood the user's problems, you should start defining the requirements. In this section I'll discuss how to define requirements, how much detail should be provided in the definition, and how to make sure your requirements are complete.

GENERAL AND SPECIFIC

One of the best ways to articulate a set of requirements for a project is to create an outline. At the highest level of the outline are the general requirements. General requirements unite a collection of specific feature requirements so they can be discussed, evaluated, compared, and approved as a group. You should be able to review the general requirements of the project and get an excellent understanding of its major objectives. You shouldn't have too many general requirements because each one will generate many supporting requirements. For example, a company that wants to leverage its existing order processing application for the Internet might need only five general requirements:

◆   Offer a browser interface for the order entry application.

◆   Increase the performance so that it will be acceptable to Web users.

◆   Provide e-mail notification of the order's fulfillment.

◆   Add new features that will make the user more productive.

◆   Anticipate the future use of PDAs as a client platform.

Each general requirement should be further divided into specific requirements. Specific requirements can have other requirements associated with them that further outline or explain the parent requirement's functionality. The resulting documentation would look like this:

General Requirement 1

   Specific Requirement 1

      Sub-Requirement 1.1

      Sub-Requirement 1.2

   Specific Requirement 2

      Sub-Requirement 2.1

      Sub-Requirement 2.2

On the next page is an example of some specific and general requirements for the scenario described above.

Offer a browser interface for our order entry application.

    Functional requirements:

        Submit order:

            Require the following information (X, Y, Z) for each order.

            Validate the customer ID.

        Delete order.

        Review order status.

        Generate order confirmation.

    Browser support requirements:

        Microsoft Internet Explorer version X

        Netscape version Y

Performance must be acceptable to a Web user.

    Response time requirements:

        Submitting an order should take less than three seconds.

        Deleting an order should take less than six seconds.

        Reviewing order status should take less than four seconds.

        Confirming an order should take less than half an hour.

Make the application easier to use by offering new features.

    Allow the user to request multiple products with a single order.

    Allow the user to look up their customer ID.

As you can see, each general requirement has a set of supporting requirements that further extend or explain the parent requirement. Each supporting requirement is simple and clear; it can be easily tracked throughout the release. You should continue to add more detailed specifications until you're comfortable that you have described all the key elements of the feature.

COMPLETENESS

Your requirement definition needs to be complete. Consider every aspect of the release—even those that don't translate into many smaller requirements. The following list contains some common requirement categories that affect almost all software projects. I'm not suggesting that you use this as an outline for your requirements—although you could—but you should consider each category when you write your requirements.

◆   *Tasks and features*   Everyone on the team needs to understand what the key tasks and features are before they begin working on the project. These tasks and features will be the essence of the release and will drive the development, quality assurance, and user education effort.

◆   *User interface*   Although the two big UI questions, "How does the user do X?" and "What does feature Y look like?" need to be answered, it's best not to try to write out these requirements. It's just too difficult to describe, test, and iterate improvements. Instead, you should employ user interface prototyping techniques to develop a visual model of your application. This model will become your user interface requirements specification. (In Chapter 9, I discuss this topic in detail and explain how you can effectively define and validate your product's UI requirements.) However, if there are specific platform, technology, or business constraints that will affect the user interface design, it's important that you articulate them up front.

◆   *Environment*   Describe the software and hardware environment in which the product will work. This description should clearly indicate the specific versions of the existing software and hardware and anticipate new releases that might be available. You should also consider globalization issues such as operating system support, local language support, and currency and time differences.

◆   *Integration*   Define any integration or interoperability needs with existing software or hardware products. If you need to integrate, specify how the integration should work and which versions of the software or hardware will be supported.

◆   *Performance*   Define the product's performance expectations. State in simple terms the goals and an appropriate way to measure them.

You should consider such topics as response times under specific types of loads or demands.

◆   *Installation*   Account for the software's installation. At minimum, the definition of the requirements should discuss the steps the user would perform to install the software, the steps the installation procedure itself would take to complete the installation process, and the platforms the installation procedure needs to support.

◆   *Quality assurance*   Requirements that support the QA effort can be extremely valuable as well as a boon to productivity. For example, if your installation procedure had a mode that required no manual input, you would be able to automatically install and test the daily build. You might also want the product to support a set of APIs that allow the test team to read any binary files used or produced by the product, which would allow you to compare these files between runs of the regression test beds. You could also have the product create a log file of all internal inconsistencies as it runs, which would help the development team diagnose strange behavior that is hard to reproduce.

Detail

One of the issues that you will need to resolve is the amount of detail that should be included in the requirement definition. Certainly your goal is to provide as much definition as possible—the more you know, the better you'll be able to track your progress. With more up-front definition, your QA, user education, and release teams can work in parallel with the engineers in the development of the software because they will have a good understanding of what is being built. However, it's often difficult if not impossible to provide a sufficient level of detail in the requirements documentation, because (as is the case with most software projects) you are likely working in areas that are not familiar to you. You need to experiment and try new ideas before you can understand what you are trying to build. It might even turn out that it's not possible for you to build it at all. The following section offers one way to bridge the need to experiment and the need to document your project's requirements.

Acknowledge that insufficient detail usually means there's insufficient understanding. If the missing information involves marketing or business issues, there's not much the development team can do—this is the work of the project manager and the product manager. However, if the missing information involves feature implementation questions such as how the feature works, where the information comes from, or what the user wants, you can create a user interface prototype that explains what these features look like externally. If the missing information involves technical capabilities such as whether or not your product can perform certain tasks, you can perform a technical feasibility analysis and create a prototype. Figure 8-1 shows how to incorporate real-world results, experimentation, and creativity into the requirements process before you commit to a schedule.

FIGURE 8-1   *Relationship between requirements, usability, and prototyping*

The main idea is to learn where you have the most risk and to develop potential solutions to the problems before the project starts in earnest. Feasibility analysis and UI prototypes will help you understand your problems, evaluate your needs, and reduce the overall risk. They provide real-world feedback into the requirements definition process and will help you provide greater detail for your planning effort.

In Chapters 9 and 10, I'll describe the basic techniques of technical risk analysis and user interface prototyping, and how you can use them to create better requirements.

ASSESSING THE REQUIREMENTS

After the requirements have been defined but before they have been approved, it's wise to review them individually and collectively. You must be very selective about the requirements you put into your release. Many teams simply collect a set of requirements without analyzing their individual or collective commercial appeal and weeding out what does not fit the vision of the release. The release often becomes fragmented and lacks consistency of purpose. Take time to access your requirements and find out where your release is headed.

REQUIREMENT FRAGMENTATION

It is very easy to develop a set of requirements that emphasizes areas you might not have intended. This can happen when a group of people—or one strong-willed individual—alters the focus of the requirements in a way that you did not intend. Perhaps it was easier to develop requirements on features that were the simplest to define, or you might have found that your requirements were too risky for the type of release you wanted. Regardless, you must be sure to take an objective look at the requirements and evaluate their overall impact.

REQUIREMENT CATEGORIES

The following is a simple description of four kinds of requirements:

◆ *"Go-ahead" vs. "catch-up" requirements*   A go-ahead requirement puts your product ahead of your competitors in the marketplace. A go-ahead requirement could be as simple as the addition of new views of data or the ability to support a new platform. It doesn't have to be revolutionary; it just has to give you a competitive advantage when the release is delivered. A catch-up requirement brings your features in line with those of your competitor. Catch-up requirements are essential for staying competitive and addressing immediate issues from a sales and support point of view.

  The go-ahead / catch-up assessment can help you understand the competitive nature of your release. For example, you may find you don't have enough (or any) go-ahead requirements, and you might decide to add more. At NuMega, our release strategy always called for some features to make it unique in the market and to achieve or remain "best of breed."

◆ *Backward-looking vs. forward-looking requirements*   Backward-looking requirements address issues or problems with previous releases of the software. For example, issues with the product's past performance and usability would generally be addressed with backward-looking requirements. Because they are reactions to the existing product in the existing environment, they improve the product but do not anticipate future needs.

Forward-looking requirements anticipate the future needs of the customer. These requirements are based on the belief that customer needs or desires will be changing—even if the customers themselves don't know it yet. Forward-looking requirements are often based on major changes in business practices (use of the Web for placing orders, for example), changes in technology (like the introduction of wireless platforms), or changes in the market (like a merger of two competitors). Forward-looking requirements are the most difficult to develop; however, if you anticipate the customer needs correctly and are in the right market with the right features, you'll have a considerable advantage.

You need to make sure you have an appropriate blend of backward-looking and forward-looking requirements that meets the needs for your product, market, and release goals. For example, you might want to have a short six-month release in which to address a number of backward-looking requirements while simultaneously maintaining a few forward-looking requirements to address an interesting opportunity.

Keep in mind that forward-looking requirements are not necessarily the same as go-ahead requirements. A forward-looking requirement *anticipates* a need, but a go-ahead requirement can be based on current needs that are simply not being met by any other competitor. For example, the introduction of charts and graphics or a new one-step data entry process could be considered go-ahead features, but they wouldn't be considered forward-looking. On the other hand, the support of a PDA platform might be considered both a go-ahead and a forward-looking requirement—a double benefit.

A Visual Presentation

One easy way to understand your requirements collectively is to chart them in a four-quadrant requirements assessment grid. Figure 8-2 on the next page is a four-quadrant grid showing catch-up and go-ahead on one axis and forward-looking and backward-looking on another.

	Catch-up	Go-ahead
Forward-looking	2	1
Backward-looking	4	3

FIGURE 8-2   *Requirements charted as a four-quadrant grid*

The following are descriptions of each quadrant. When you place your own requirements in the quadrants it should become clear how your release is shaping up.

Quadrant 1   You are anticipating future needs and will be the first vendor to provide a solution. These needs might not be well understood or established; you are breaking new ground, so your risk level is quite high. Because there are so many unknowns, you won't be able to provide a lot of up-front definition. You'll need to place an emphasis on iterative prototyping. You will need to iterate your designs very quickly, employ real users to test them, and update your requirements before entering a scheduling stage.

Quadrant 2   Your competitors have a set of features that anticipate customer needs and you want to catch up with them. Research their offering, understand what they did right and what they did wrong, and exploit their mistakes. Your risks should be less in this quadrant than they are in quadrant 1 because there is already an existing product to learn from. However, market and customer needs are likely to be changing rapidly, and you'll need to perform a lot of prototyping of usability and technical designs before formalizing the requirements and establishing a schedule.

Quadrant 3   This just might be one of the best to find yourself in— delivering a set of features that will be unique in the industry without the risk of incorrectly anticipating market trends. Because you are working with a well-known or established customer, the risks for this type of release are usually associated with correct feature implementation and timely delivery rather than technology innovation.

Quadrant 4   In this tactical release, you're adding features to a product that your competitor already has shipped. The risk for this release should be relatively small because you are working on features and technology that should already be understood for a market that has already been established. Because this type of release has so little risk, it should not require as much usability testing and prototyping iteration as the others.

Remember, the goal of this exercise is to make sure your requirements will have the commercial impact you desire. Although it's possible to have a set of requirements that are equally divided among the four quadrants, that is generally not advisable, because you could end up with a release that is lacking a clear vision or focus. It is far better to have the majority of your requirements in one quadrant and supported by fewer requirements in one or two other quadrants.

PRIORITIZING THE REQUIREMENTS

With the requirements defined and the assessment complete, you are very close to having a solid set of features. Before you move forward, however, you need to prioritize the features. Prioritization helps you understand ahead of time how important each feature is and how it relates to other requirements.

WHY IT'S IMPORTANT

Prioritization directs the scheduling and assignment of tasks. In general, you want to schedule the most critical requirements for completion as early as possible. When the entire team is focused on completing the most important requirements first, the unknown risks inherent in any schedule are mitigated. Once all the critical features are complete, you have a viable release. If you run into any scheduling pressures or unanticipated changes after that point, you will be in a good position to get the release out quickly because the essential features are already complete.

The team must agree up front on the priority level of each requirement. If and when the time comes that you have to make hard decisions about which feature will get cut, you don't want the pressure of the moment and the emotions that often surface influencing the decision-making process. There must not be any confusion about which features are essential and which features are optional. Every member needs to have an understanding of feature priorities for the release.

How to Do It

Assign each requirement a priority. In this way, you can provide whatever level of specification is necessary. Priorities are defined as follows:

- *Must-have*   A must-have requirement is one that is essential to the release; you cannot release the product without it. Must-have features are implemented and tested as early as possible. They command the full attention and resources of the project.

- *Should-have*   A should-have requirement is one that is highly desirable. You could, with proper justification, back the requirement out of the release, but it is very important that you deliver these features. Should-have requirements are implemented and tested immediately after must-have requirements.

- *Could-have*   A could-have requirement is one that is desirable but will be one of the last to be implemented and the first to be reviewed for exclusion should scheduling problems surface.

Approving the Requirements

Many teams mistakenly think that after the requirements have been defined, they are ready to assign tasks and schedule the project. Instead, you need to complete two other important steps: conduct a technical evaluation of key technology risks, and create a user interface prototype for your software. These topics will be covered in the next two chapters.

Let's assume for the moment that you have completed a user interface prototype and a technological assessment. Are you ready to sign off on your requirements? Not yet. You shouldn't sign off on the requirements until the schedule is done. You might find that the schedule is too long and you need to cut back on some requirements. If you have already signed off on the requirements, you might find that they cannot possibly be satisfied in the time frame you want. Don't commit to one requirement without being sure of the others.

Managing Change

Software development is a dynamic process. No matter how great your initial requirements are, you are going to need to make changes to them as your development cycle progresses. Unexpected problems will surface, new ideas will be proposed, and market needs will change. The fact that requirements are changing is not the most important concern, however. The most important concern is that you have a process that helps raise these issues for review, guide your decision making, and communicate the result to the team.

Here are the fundamental principles you need to consider:

◆ *Establish a team comprised of the project manager and all leads to review all changes.* This team should meet regularly, be very responsive to change requests, and ensure that each team lead gets the opportunity to review the impact of the change. The project manager should make sure the change request process is efficient and appropriate for the team. The project manager must also review the impact on the schedule. If a change is going to be made, the schedule should be reviewed and changed if necessary.

◆ *Feature teams should be allowed, if not encouraged, to improve their features.* This freedom will allow quick iteration and improvement to the product. However, you must not allow these detailed, fine-tuning improvements to negatively impact the schedule. If the change affects the requirements or will take more time than the schedule allows, be sure to follow the change request process described earlier.

The only exception, however, involves must-have requirements. They are the most important and as such they cannot be changed without additional external review and approval. Other parts of the company are depending on the delivery of these features and should be part of the decision-making process as well. For example, external reviews would involve product management, marketing, senior management, and other key stakeholders.

◆ *Communicate all changes to the entire team.* It can be as simple as sending an e-mail to the team or talking through a set of changes at a status meeting. Just make sure everyone is notified of the change.

◆ *Document all changes.* This documentation allows the team to review and track changes that have been made over the course of the project. You should provide the date of the change, the nature of the change, and a short justification. It's important to have a single repository for this information over the life of the release so team members can refer to this information as needed. You could maintain a change history at the top of the requirement document to show a record of changes or you could log all approved change orders sent to a specific distribution list.

COMMON PROBLEMS AND SOLUTIONS

The following are some of the typical problems and questions that surface when applying these techniques, and some solutions to those problems.

FINDING THE TIME

One of the most common objections to the requirements definition (and the UI prototyping effort that follows) is the amount of time these tasks take. Some people might look at this time and wonder if it's well spent. At the beginning of a project, there's pressure to show results, so it's easy to wonder if you should spend valuable time defining requirements.

The answer to this question is simply "yes." Some approaches to software development would have you take a lot of time performing a detailed requirements definition and analysis, but the approach I've outlined here (and will expand on in the next two chapters) offers a cycle of requirements definition supported by real-world experimentation and feedback. This keeps the entire team engaged and allows creativity and experimentation before schedules are drafted and commitments are made. In addition, the UI and technical prototyping provide visible, tangible results of the progress being made.

DESCRIBING WHAT—NOT HOW

Requirements specifications should define what needs to be done but not how to do it. The "how" is best answered through technology feasibility and feature and UI prototyping. Unfortunately, many teams place how statements in their requirements specification, which can limit the number of possible solutions. Instead, let the creativity of the team generate multiple solutions, and then try them out with real-world experimentation.

Let's take a UI example for the order processing application described earlier. One of the key requirements should be, "Accept product orders by capturing the following information: X, Y, and Z." Notice that this requirement states what needs to be done but does not state how to do it. An example of a "how" requirement might be, "The user selects the New | Create Order menu item and enters the information into a dialog box." Let the UI team determine the best way to satisfy this requirement through UI prototyping.

MISSING ESSENTIALS

Most projects struggle with requirements because they lack requirements management. They suffer from unfocused and incomplete requirements, no prioritization, or no change management process. This chapter focused only on the essentials—the "must haves" to maintain control and predictability in the project without overburdening the team with process and paperwork. Don't leave any of these out of your project.

9 Research, Evaluation, and Prototyping

At the beginning of any high-pressure project, there is a tremendous temptation to make assumptions about key technical elements of your project. These assumptions might be about using new technologies, new components, or new platforms. They could be assumptions about the performance or scalability of the project's architecture or even the suitability of the development environment and tools. If you make the right assumptions, you're going to save a lot of time and be a big hero. But if you make the wrong assumptions, you might find yourself doomed from the start.

Does this mean that all projects are a crapshoot? In many ways, yes, that's exactly what they are. Without some understanding of the planning issues I address in this chapter, you are taking a huge risk. Sometimes it will work out, but most of the time it won't. Why? Simply because the odds are against you—the more assumptions you make, the more risk you incur.

Wouldn't it be great if there were a way to increase your chances of making the right assumptions? Wouldn't it be even better if you could verify your key assumptions before you committed to a final delivery date? Well, there is. In this chapter, I'll discuss how research, technology evaluation, and prototyping can help you verify your assumptions and keep a project on track.

THE BENEFITS

Research, evaluation, and prototyping help you understand—before you start a project—the capabilities and limitations of the technologies you plan to use. By making full use of these approaches, you will be better able to:

- *Manage risk and create good schedules.* You need to identify your project's major technology issues and figure out a way to address them early in the project. As I've mentioned previously, unresolved technology issues can play havoc with schedules. In fact, it's one of the top causes of major schedule slips. You shouldn't commit to a schedule or start a project in earnest until key technology issues have been resolved.

- *Build confidence.* When first working with new technologies, new approaches, or new architectures, a team's confidence that everything will work can be quite low. This is understandable; no one has experience with these issues, and the chances of success can seem quite poor. This doubt, however, can cause real problems. If your team doesn't have confidence that their project will succeed, morale and productivity can suffer. The goal is to eliminate this doubt as early as possible and build the team's confidence so the project can and will be successful.

◆   *Anticipate performance problems.* Most people realize that application performance is becoming more and more important. Unfortunately, true performance tuning is not something you can leave until the end of a project and then optimize. Instead, you need to build a model of your key software architecture up front and test it as early as possible to find out how well your design scales.

◆   *Create technological breakthroughs.* In any competitive market you must do research. You must devote some portion of your staff's time to anticipating consumer needs and finding breakthrough ideas or solutions. Great ideas, new approaches, and killer apps don't happen by magic. They need to be nurtured over time.

RESEARCH

Although some people might think of research as being an academic pursuit, research also plays an important role in product development. In this section, I'll discuss research basics and their application to your product initiatives.

WHAT IS IT?

Research comes in two forms: *pure research* and *applied research*. Pure research is a process of discovery and invention in the hope of creating something useful. However, that creation does not always have a commercial application. Applied research, on the other hand, looks at what is happening in a particular industry, makes logical guesses at what solutions might be beneficial, and tries to transform those hypotheses into concrete product ideas.

Applied research is the most important form of research for the purposes of this book. It can provide critical competitive advantages—especially during market disruptions, when the needs of users as well as hardware and software platforms or technologies are going through sweeping changes. Although these changes can often bring uncertainty, they can also present incredible opportunities for the teams that can anticipate customer needs and harness the emerging technologies. If you're creating technology, you must have a sustained research effort running parallel to your development cycle if you want to stay afloat despite all the fluctuations.

Back at Work

NuMega's SoftICE kernel debugger was a big hit on the 16-bit Microsoft DOS and Microsoft Windows platforms. We even got it working on Windows 95 without too many problems. However, the market was heading toward Windows NT in a big way and we needed to get SoftICE to work for that operating system, or our future revenue growth would surely be adversely affected. But it looked like this was going to be impossible—NT's new virtual memory management system made the implementation of many of SoftICE's features extremely difficult, and many of SoftICE's commands required intimate knowledge of Windows internals and data structures that were not public. Many people inside and outside the company didn't think SoftICE could ever be ported to Windows NT.

Fortunately, we had a person, Frank Grossman, who believed that it could be done and was willing to do the research. He worked day and night for two weeks on the problem and developed a relatively simple prototype that showed the basic techniques needed to support Windows NT. Once he showed the prototype to the team, it was all over—everyone saw that we could make SoftICE work with Windows NT. Although it took almost an extra year of sophisticated development, we were able to deliver the product that they said couldn't be created. Because of this research and determination, we not only were able to grow our revenue stream significantly, but the knowledge we gained created huge barriers of entry to competitors and could be leveraged into other products.

How to Do It

The following are different ways in which you can find a balance between research and development. The first is the least resource-intensive and the last is the most resource-intensive. If you're a small company or are simply short on resources, you might want to start with the first model and grow into the other models over time.

◆ *Research projects during minor releases*   Software products tend to go in cycles—first a major release and then a minor release. Minor releases are characterized as tactical; that is, they provide additional features or improvements that refine or extend the existing feature set of a product already on the market. These releases are usually quick and less risky than major releases. Because of these characteristics, minor releases are a great way to give some of your lead developers a break from regular development and a chance to perform research. The overall goal is to complete the research when the minor release is winding down.

In addition to the research work itself, combining research with minor releases has advantages for your staff as well. The lead developers get a change of pace and a chance to work on different issues. This opportunity can really refresh your top talent and keep burnout at a minimum. It also provides an opportunity for others to perform the lead position. Cross training and allowing talent to grow are critical to preventing turnover and keeping your team's skills growing.

◆ *Alternate developer leads*   If you're fortunate enough to have two or more capable dev leads, you should consider alternating them between releases. While one is working on a release, the other can be researching new technologies and ideas. When the product has been released, they swap positions. The developer who has been doing research brings enthusiasm and the knowledge learned during the research cycle to the team, and the other developer looks forward to performing the next set of research work.

◆ *Dedicated research leads*   As your products increase in complexity, size, or number, it is likely that you'll need an ongoing research effort. In this scenario, you should consider recruiting or assigning top-tier individuals to ongoing research projects. These individuals, in addition to having an excellent work ethic and the ability to think and work independently, must also have excellent communication skills. They need to be a part of the product team without working on a day-to-day basis with the team. This arrangement can work out very well, or it can lead to estrangement between the team and the researchers. It's up to the individuals themselves and the project manager to make sure this doesn't happen. Regular communication, both formal and informal, can reduce the chance of creating divisions between teams.

One of the remaining questions I need to address is how to focus the research effort. If you're in a small resource environment, you must make sure your research has the highest chance of success. You need to invest your effort wisely. In general, you want to focus your effort on the following opportunities:

- *Market trends and advances*   Every three or four years, the market introduces new technological advances. Whether they relate to graphical user interfaces, client/server development, component object models, or the Internet, you must stay abreast of these fundamental changes and not be left behind as major changes are taking place. Use your research effort to look for, understand, and track major market moves. Don't get so lost in your own effort that you ignore the greater context around you.

- *New ideas*   New product or technological ideas can come at any time and from anywhere. Sometimes they come from internal sources and other times they come from external ones. Some could be worth millions of dollars and others could be a big waste of time. Your research effort should be skilled at taking these new ideas and quickly separating the good ones from the bad ones.

- *Competitor innovations and directions*   One of the most important areas to focus research on is that of competitor innovations and directions. You need to understand your competitors' technology, strengths, and weaknesses to compete against them successfully.

When you complete research projects or your priorities change, it's important to document and share the results. The information learned in research projects—both the successes and failures—should be communicated back to the team. If a research project is showing real potential, it's often wise to have a prototype available to show the team what the research project can do and how it works.

Back at Work

Toward the end of the BoundsChecker 3.0 project, our dev lead's enthusiasm was waning—the project had been long and hard, and it was clear to everyone on the team that a change was needed. At the same time, we needed to understand how a hot new technology from Microsoft called COM would impact our products. It was getting a lot of attention and appeared to be "the way of the future," but we had little idea what it was about. So we decided to solve both problems at the same time.

While the rest of the team was working on the product's next (minor) release, we assigned our dev lead a full-time research project to learn the internal workings of COM and to prototype new feature ideas for BoundsChecker. After three months, the minor release was essentially complete, and our dev lead was ready to join the BoundsChecker 4.0 effort. In addition to being refreshed, he was able to educate the rest of the team on COM and present working feature prototypes. As a startup, we were well positioned. We were shipping 3.0, had just finished 3.1, and we had the fundamental technology we needed to drive our next major release.

TECHNOLOGY EVALUATION

Before you set out on your next project, be sure you understand the technology you are going to use—especially on projects that introduce new software tools, components, platforms, or solutions. In this section, I'll discuss why and how to do technical evaluations.

WHAT IS IT?

Almost all software development projects today rely on other technologies. A typical Web application now uses operating system features, graphic libraries, third-party components, Web servers, transactions servers, and database servers. You will need to understand the capabilities of one or all of these technologies. Before you start your project, you need to evaluate whether the capabilities of any new technology will fit your project's needs. An evaluation provides you with a hands-on forum to test and resolve open issues. You might even find new problems that you never knew existed until you started using the technology.

It's amazing how often teams are willing to make assumptions when it comes to new technology—or at a minimum, proceed based on what they read in the press or in a newsgroup. Every team needs to evaluate every piece of new technology that it is introducing into the project. If your project is using a lot of new technology (either new to market or new to the team) you need to spend some time with it before you start your project.

How to Do It

When you evaluate technology, consider the following:

- *Capability*   Does it have the features you need for your project?

- *Quality*   Does the technology have the quality you need?

- *Sophistication*   Does the technology have the performance, scalability, and robustness you need?

- *Support*   Is the technology adequately supported?

- *Ease of use*   Is the technology easy to use and to debug?

- *Team skills*   Does your team have the skills to use this technology?

Technology evaluations are actually quite simple from a process point of view, but you need to execute them relatively quickly—after all, you're gating the release of your final schedule based on the result of your evaluation. Even though you don't have the luxury of a lot of time, the following are some key steps you should consider for all your evaluation projects:

- *Define your criteria.* Define your needs as best you can up front, based on the technology evaluation criteria just given.

- *Measure against your criteria.* Measure the results objectively—with facts and not opinions.

- *Get customer references.* Be sure to get customer references to validate your results—both positive and negative—and be sure to ask them about their own evaluation projects and how well the technology met their needs.

PROTOTYPES

At the beginning of a project there will almost always be important questions about technology implementation. Prototyping is an important technique to provide you with the answers that you need.

WHAT IS IT?

Prototyping is one of the most essential steps any software team can take before it begins a project. Prototyping helps you understand how to effectively implement key features, estimate the complexity and duration of key technology efforts, and minimize the overall risk of a faulty or lengthy implementation.

Let's take a look at what can happen without prototyping. After identifying all the components of a project, one of the first pieces of software the team decides to build is the infrastructure. This is often the most critical and sophisticated component, so the team decides to build it first because nothing else can work without it. Without doing any prototyping, this component is designed and built. Once this is complete, the team decides to layer the other components around it. But after these newer components are integrated, the infrastructure is discovered to be insufficient, poorly designed, or incapable of being scaled. So you begin to look at what went wrong, and you design new solutions and start coding again. At this point, you are iterating the software's design in your code and doing it during the development cycle, which will obviously cause delays to the schedule and the delivery of the software.

Let's take another example, this time using an opposite scenario. Your team recognizes that it can't build a project's infrastructure components without understanding the technical requirements of the rest of the system. The team decides to spec the entire system, but they find this task is difficult because they don't know all the issues they need to address ahead of time. In fact, there are many big questions, and no one really knows what the answers are. You can guess and hope to get it all right—but that's very risky.

Prototyping can help you solve these problems. In the first example, prototyping could have helped you model the entire system earlier so that you'd know how all the components should fit together. In the second example, prototyping could have provided the data you needed to help drive your engineering plans.

Back at Work

Both of the examples just discussed occurred in real projects. In the early days at NuMega, we did not consistently prototype the technology that had the highest risk or uncertainty. But looking back, if we had simply done up-front design and certified it with proper prototyping, we could have avoided these problems.

How to Do It

Prototyping isn't an opportunity to write an entire application—it's an opportunity to get facts to help you make better decisions. Time is of the essence so you need to move quickly. The following is the shortest path through a solid prototyping effort:

♦   *Identify key risks.* The first step is to list the major questions you need to answer. You should consider any topic that you need to understand in order to develop an accurate schedule. If you have many issues, prioritize them and work out the most important ones first. Remember to focus primarily on key areas, not every unknown area.

♦   *Define experiments.* Develop some experiments that will help you find the answers to these questions. You could have a different experiment for each issue, or you could group your experiments together to solve multiple problems.

No matter how many experiments you have, you need to prototype the integration of any key technology or component. This activity links the crucial parts of the system together to perform a set of important tasks all the way throughout the system. The goal here is to work through the product broadly but not deeply. I can't tell you how many times I've seen or heard of projects that have catastrophic problems getting all the pieces to work together, when some system-level prototyping would have uncovered these problems within the first couple of weeks of the project.

◆ *Simulate end result.* One of the keys to getting your prototyping work done is to simulate the end result. You need to travel through time, take a peek at what the end state of your product will look like, and try to model the essential pieces up front. To do this successfully, you need to take shortcuts. You might need to define a set of temporary components and APIs and wire them together to create a simulation. You might be required to hard wire certain function calls, stub out others, and provide placeholder data. This is all okay because you're only building a simulator. Your goal is to create a skeleton and add meat later.

◆ *Leverage existing technology.* Another important way to accelerate prototyping is to leverage existing technology. You don't need to do everything from scratch. Some of the most successful prototyping efforts are the result of taking a copy of the production source code and hacking it up.

◆ *Evaluate what you have done.* After you have the prototype, don't forget to evaluate your results. You might want to understand macro-level performance, memory utilization, or memory footprint. You might want to consider ease of implementation and the quality of the technology, and you might want to understand how the technology works or is created. Whatever your needs, get as much value as you can from the prototype.

◆ *Document the result with design notes.* Document your results. This step benefits not only current team members, but also future members. If you have discovered critical issues during the prototyping process, the issues are likely to come up again in the future. Everyone on the team should know why important decisions were made. Over time you'll develop a library of design notes that will provide historical documentation for your project.

Back at Work

At NuMega, our BoundsChecker 5.0 effort required a major rewrite of the internal components of our product. The rewrite was primarily divided into two parts: collecting information and analyzing information. Because of the complexity of the project, it was very tempting to fully design the collection side, and then do the same to the analysis side. But because the project was so complex, we felt that it was more important to prototype each side at the same time instead of writing lengthy specs. We decided that we would collect a subset of the data and write just the analysis code that would be applicable for that data. If this worked, we'd display a simple dialog box saying it worked.

After a week's worth of work, a developer on the team called me into his office and showed me that simple little dialog box. It worked! We knew that it would now be possible to do what we wanted—end to end—and that the performance would not be a huge issue. Over the next two weeks, we started scaling the feature set one step at a time, gaining more knowledge and confidence, and making our final architecture and designs more solid. After three weeks, we had a proven design that we could accurately schedule, and it made a huge difference in bringing the project in on time. I'm not suggesting things were perfect thereafter. But without these simple steps, we would not have had the confidence, background, or understanding to make accurate plans.

COMMON PROBLEMS AND SOLUTIONS

The following are some of the typical problems and questions that surface when applying these techniques, and some solutions to those problems.

WINGING IT

As I've mentioned frequently in this chapter, teams often make assumptions about new technology. These assumptions make the execution of the project more like gambling than engineering. Don't just wing it. Although you'll need to take some issues at face value, you should define your key needs and verify that the new technology satisfies them. You will be better prepared for anticipated issues and be able to react to them earlier in a project development cycle rather than later.

PROTOTYPING IN ISOLATION

It's often tempting to prototype components independently of their usage or context. Although it's much easier to focus on a smaller portion, it can be very dangerous. Prototyping shouldn't focus on just one component of the project, it should focus on the integration and interaction between critical shared components. I strongly recommend a system-wide prototype that brings the critical pieces together even if data is contrived and APIs are hardwired or stubbed out. You'll still get a good idea of the integration issues and prove that the system-level design is valid.

ANALYZING PERFORMANCE TOO LATE

Most people think that performance is added to the software at the end of the project development cycle. Although it's certainly true that the optimizations can and should be made after the whole project is assembled, it's also true that you are quite limited in the amount of change you can make. You are certainly in no position to fundamentally alter the architecture or internal structure of the product as you're heading into the final weeks of the schedule.

Macro-level performance analysis must be done up front—first on prototypes, and again later as the software comes together, in base levels and at milestones.

10

User Interface

Almost all team members understand that a great user interface (UI) is key to their product's success. Unfortunately, that's where the agreement ends. Often, teams that struggle with UI problems either have no process for prototyping their UI or simply cannot agree on what that process should be. UI issues can often provide the most significant challenges to keeping a project on schedule.

If your team is like most, some of the most hotly debated issues are about the UI—what it should do, how it should work, and what it should look like. These debates can sometimes last for an entire project and cause infighting, delays, and false starts. To make matters worse, you can easily be surprised late in a project by UI problems that you never anticipated. At that point, any change requires a lot of rework by the development, QA, and documentation teams. You're talking about a major schedule slip.

The solution to this problem is to develop a prototype of the UI early in the development cycle. Test it, evaluate it, and improve it as rapidly as possible until you have resolved major issues. In this chapter, I'll discuss the importance of having a UI prototype and how to create one for virtually any project. I won't cover what constitutes a good UI because this can vary greatly between platforms. Instead I'll cover how to introduce an effective but lightweight UI process into your software development cycle without the need for high-end facilities, specialized resources, and lengthy time commitments. Finally, I'll discuss the role of the human factors engineer and show how this key individual can drive the UI effort for the team.

WHAT IS A UI PROTOTYPE?

A UI prototype is a visual representation of your UI. It is essentially a working draft of what you think your users want, as well as a representation of what you think you need to build. Your prototype can take many different forms, from paper prototypes to actual software mock-ups. (I'll discuss how to create a prototype later.) However, no matter which form your prototype takes, it should show the development team how users will interact with the software.

WHY IS IT NEEDED?

As I discussed in Chapter 8, the product requirements define the major tasks users need to perform. However, the requirement specification does not define how users will perform these tasks; the UI prototype does. The product team and, more specifically, the human factors engineer perform this work. Once your prototype is available, you should be able to validate the chosen implementation details by having users test them to make sure you've got them right. And most importantly, you should be able to make changes easily and try new ideas based on the feedback that you receive from your software tests.

A UI prototype provides many advantages to the development team and the development effort. These include:

◆   *Focusing on key tasks*   You need to focus the team's efforts on the most important parts of the product. The most important parts of the product are the key tasks that the user values the most, uses the most, or appreciates the most. Your entire team—development, QA, tech writing, and so on—must identify exactly what these key tasks are and work very hard to get these tasks right. To some extent, the rest of the product doesn't matter if these basic tasks are not easy and intuitive.

Back at Work

At NuMega, when we decided to build a new profiler product, TrueTime, we knew that we had to create a new UI from scratch. But what would it look like? What would be the most important things users would want to do? We looked around the industry and found that there were many good products sporting a very mature product set. But all of the products overloaded users with data. We thought this was a disadvantage because it made the most important task of the product—easily finding a product's performance problem—very difficult. From that moment on our focus was clear: Our product would allow users to "find performance problems in three clicks or less." Our entire team worked together to make sure that the UI supported this straightforward yet difficult-to-achieve goal. Our solution was to keep the UI very simple, but to create a new approach to navigating through the complex call hierarchies in which performance problems often lurk. How did this work out? Well, our first release won the Comdex/Byte Magazine "Best of Show" award—largely due to the focus the development team had on a single set of issues.

◆   *Accuracy*   As I mentioned earlier in this chapter, one of the biggest problems with product development is the rework that can result from redesigning and reimplementing the UI over and over and over. You must eliminate major reworks to stay on schedule. Although it's virtually impossible to get a product perfect the first time, major elements of the UI must be nailed down early. Minor changes might be okay, but major changes can be disastrous because of the impact on development time, product quality, and documentation.

◆   *Scheduling*   You can't schedule accurately if you don't know what the UI will be. In fact, if you decide to have the UI evolve throughout the development cycle, you'll need your schedule to evolve in the same way. You must also guard against a *strung out* schedule. This occurs when all the quality and tech writing efforts are delayed by an evolving UI and thereby delay the overall length of the project. Remember, you should be running all parts of the project in parallel with the development of the software. Scheduling requires that the UI be well understood at the start of the project.

◆   *Documentation*   You must have documentation that describes how to use the software. Obviously, the product's documentation is heavily dependent on the UI. The writing teams need to know what problems users will encounter and how the software helps solve those problems. If the UI is not solid at the beginning of the project, the writing effort will constantly be in catch-up mode and will not run in parallel to the product's development.

◆   *Testing*   The testing effort is also heavily dependent on the UI. Traditionally, the QA team asks the developers for a detailed, functional spec to describe the exact behavior of the product. Unfortunately, it's almost impossible to fully describe a UI—especially modern UIs. Instead, it's best to create a prototype. If the QA team could experience the product through the UI prototype and understand the fundamentals of the end-user features and how

those features work, they could create much better test plans. I
don't mean to imply that a description of the features is not important or that it shouldn't occur, but I want to emphasize that one
of the best ways of illustrating product information is through the
prototype. With a UI prototype in place, a QA team knows the
core paths through the product. Because the team understands
how the product features work, they can build better test plans
and test beds before the software is even finished.

How Is It Developed?

By now you are probably saying, "This sounds great, but how is it done?"
NuMega's approach to developing a UI was based on three simple concepts.
First, we identified the most important tasks that users needed to perform.
Second, we quickly modeled these tasks early in the project—before we committed to a final schedule—so that we'd have a better chance of correctly
estimating the work we had ahead of us. Lastly, we iterated the prototype very quickly, showing it both internally and externally, so that we
could validate it with users. The ability to iterate quickly was the key to
success and allowed us to finalize our prototype as early as possible.

When your team completes these three tasks, you'll have a UI prototype that everyone on the team understands before the product is built. Think
about what this means. The developers, test engineers, and tech writers will
all have an excellent idea of what the product will look like before the project
is ever built. Think how much more productive and efficient everyone on the
team will be with a UI prototype in place. In addition, executive management, product management, marketing, and technical support will also see
the product before it's built. This exposure will create a great deal of excitement, confidence, and anticipation—that high-tech buzz that you need to get
everyone going in one direction. And let's not forget the most important
point—by validating your UI up front, you should have a better chance of
having a great product because it's been seen and used by many people
before it's even been built.

Clearly, these steps sound ideal, and they can be accomplished with the appropriate effort and skills. Let's take a closer look at each of the three steps.

Identifying Key Tasks

The first step in identifying a UI is to identify the most important tasks users want to perform. The number of tasks can vary based on the complexity of the product, but look for tasks that fall into these two categories:

◆ *Tasks new users most likely want to perform*   The goal is to understand the needs of first-time users and make sure that your product helps them be successful as soon as possible. The product must not frustrate the users, but rather encourage them to use the product more. If you know what users are likely to do, you can optimize the UI for their needs.

◆ *Tasks regular users most frequently want to perform*   The goal is to keep regular users happy by identifying the key tasks they use. If you can get these right, you have a great chance of satisfying users over the long term. Accordingly, you want these tasks to receive the most attention from the development team. They should be very feature rich, high quality, and well documented.

Prototyping

With the tasks identified, you are in a good position to start creating the UI prototype. The selection of your prototyping tool is very important. You need to be able to create a prototype quickly and easily. You'll then need to test your design ideas, fix any problems, and quickly test them again. Let's take a look at the most popular prototyping techniques and see how they might fit your needs. The following is a list of techniques from the best to the worst:

◆ *Paper prototypes*   To create a paper prototype, simply draw the UI on pieces of paper. To make this process easy for designers and users, each user artifact has its own piece of paper cut to an appropriate size. Draw and arrange the menu bars, toolbars, command buttons, list boxes, and so forth to match the UI. For example, each menu drop-down list has its own piece of paper.

Each dialog box has its own piece of paper as well. The pieces of paper don't have to be exact; they just have to make it clear what the UI elements are.

The advantage of a paper prototype is the ease with which it can be assembled and changed. By isolating the major pieces of the UI, you can easily change the flow of control, the terms, or the location or size of the UI elements. It's easy to erase lines or even redraw an entire page of the prototype. In fact, because a paper prototype is so easy to change, it can be updated and modified while it's being shown to end users, which allows you to test new ideas immediately.

Also note that a paper prototype doesn't suffer from build issues, installation issues, or other hassles that are inevitable with software development. This is an advantage because you want to spend your time testing and iterating a UI, not on the technical or mechanical issues associated with its creation.

With the introduction of more sophisticated graphics and development tools, it's getting easier to create real images of UIs and print them on paper instead of creating hand-drawn representations. Your choice should be based on personal preferences because both methods have the important qualities of simple production and quick iteration.

Back at Work

The use of paper prototypes can be extremely effective, but unless the team really believes in this technique, it might not be supported or accepted. To combat this problem at NuMega, we took the entire team to a one-day usability course offered by the Usability Engineering Institute (*www.uie.com*) that specifically emphasized paper prototyping. It was a great way to show our team how important and effective paper prototyping can be. This course changed our thoughts on how to develop software.

◆   *RAD tools*   Rapid Application Development (RAD) tools are probably the most popular way of creating prototypes. Any tool that you can use to quickly display a functioning UI will suffice.

One advantage of RAD tools is the speed with which a UI can be created (although RAD tools aren't usually as fast as paper prototypes). Another advantage is their realism. Many people think RAD tools provide a better testing experience than paper prototyping because the testing is done using real software. However, programmers can often get hung up with the coding of these prototypes and waste valuable time in assembling them. The programmers tend to iterate on the code, making the code better and not improving the actual UI. Another problem is the strong temptation to move this code directly into development even though it was never properly designed or implemented.

◆   *Specs*   UI specifications are probably the second most popular technique, but also the least valuable of the three. UI specifications suffer from three problems: First, they are often open to interpretation. It's unlikely that a detailed specification is going to be read and understood by the entire team in the same way. Second, UI specifications are hard to test and validate. It's unlikely you're going to throw a 20-page UI specification on a user's desk and ask him or her to read it. It's very hard to test against a spec. Finally, even if you do get feedback, specifications are often difficult to keep internally consistent and accurate.

Validating, Iterating, and Repeating

With your prototype in place, you are ready to test it with real users. You want users performing the key tasks you've identified using the prototype you just created. You want to learn what works well and what does not work well, and to change the prototype to address these issues.

Let's take an example using paper prototypes. If you ask the users to perform a specific task, they might need to "click" through a series of UI elements. Part of your job is to drive the mechanics of the UI, acting as a computer for the users. You'll need to put a new dialog box in front of them, watch them make their selections, and take away the dialog box when the users hit "OK."

How many times do you need to iterate? Usually a lot. You might change the design 20 times depending on the application. You should not refrain from making changes and iterating so long as you're making solid progress. Remember, the idea is to work quickly through many designs until your prototype begins to settle down. With several tests complete, you will have a good idea of how well your prototype is shaping up. Is it getting easier for people to get their work done? Is the average time users spend on a certain task decreasing or increasing? Did the last set of users encounter any problems, or have they completed the tasks quickly and easily? The answers to these questions will let you know how well you're doing and how much work you have ahead of you.

Back at Work

At NuMega, when we built our first code coverage product, TrueCoverage, we once again had to figure out what the UI would look like. To help us in this effort, our human factors engineer (who doubled as our technical writer) and our lead developer created paper prototypes of the UI. We then asked members of the team to perform tasks that we identified as the most important. As users executed these tasks, we observed their successes and failures. We also took their input and tried new approaches to solve the problems they encountered. We then took the prototype to others in the company, such as product management and technical support, to get their input. And finally, we took the prototype outside the company for real customer input. We iterated very quickly; perhaps as many as a dozen prototypes were made in a week. In fact, during our testing phase, we uncovered some major problems with our merge functionality. I hate to think how long it would have taken us to identify and fix this problem using conventional means—probably a whole release cycle or more. After a short period of time (about two weeks in all) we were able to complete the design. This is not to say that it was perfect or that there weren't minor changes later in development, but we had 90 percent of the design in place and validated by users before we started the coding of the project. A solid UI allowed us to create a schedule for the project more accurately and to have our testing and documentation teams understand, if not "use," the product before it was built.

THE ROLE OF THE HUMAN FACTORS ENGINEER

Human factors engineers play a crucial role in the development of software products. Having worked with them and without them, I'd want one (or more) on my team every time. However, the role of a human factors engineer is not always clear and varies considerably between companies. The following sections describe how we at NuMega use our human factors engineers.

OWNERSHIP

The human factors engineer's primary tasks include the following responsibilities:

- *Defining the UI prototype*   As I have discussed, the UI prototype is an integral part of a product's development. Human factors engineers drive the definition and design of the UI prototype. While this is one of their principal duties, it does not mean they work by themselves in isolation from the team or from end users. Instead, they need to lead the creation process and incorporate both their own ideas and those of the team.

- *Defining the installation prototype*   The installation is as important to a product as any other part. The installation procedure needs a UI prototype just like the rest of the software. The human factors engineers can play key roles in making sure the software is as simple to install as possible and is not burdened with complexity, customization, and manual labor.

- *Defining the Out of the Box (OOTB) experience*   One of your goals should be to make the initial experience of a product very positive. You want users to open the box, easily install the software, and be productive (able to solve a problem) in the first ten minutes of using your product. If users are successful quickly, they are far more likely to invest the time to fully learn the product and understand its power. Human factors engineers play a key role in this effort by owning, defining, and measuring the OOTB experience.

Back at Work

At NuMega, our human factors engineers improved the OOTB experience significantly by looking at all aspects of our products. They suggested that one way to improve the OOTB experience would be to include four-color quick reference cards that summarized the key tasks users would want to perform, using screen shots, call outs, and brief text descriptions. We also put basic reference information on the back of the cards to help users find key information easily. We then printed the material on high-quality wrinkle and stain resistant paper so that the cards would last through repeated use. These cards worked out so well that they were also our most popular pre-sales material.

◆ *Creating graphics, images, icons, and color schemes*   Human factors engineers should be skilled in the creation of graphical materials that will help the presentation of your software. Although human factors engineers don't necessarily have these skills, it's just one more reason to recruit multi-skilled people as often as possible.

ADVICE

The usability of software often extends beyond the software itself—it includes the packaging, licensing, and documentation of the product. Although the human factors engineers are not directly responsible for these areas, they advise the product management, marketing, and technical writing teams on many key issues, including:

◆ *Licensing*   The licensing prototype will affect users' experience of the software as well as their ultimate satisfaction. The human factors team can play key roles in the implementation of your licensing prototypes by keeping them as simple and hassle-free as possible while not compromising the goals of the product management team.

◆ *Packaging*   The packaging of the product can make a very strong impression of the product and the company that creates it. The human factors engineers can work with your product management and marketing teams to make sure you have simple, efficient, and effective packaging for your products. For NuMega, it was important that we looked as professional as possible and not appear as small as we really were.

◆ *Documentation, online help, and collateral*   Human factors engineers also play key roles in developing your documentation, online help, and collateral. They make sure these materials blend well with the product and the packaging. For example, they drive the graphics and color schemes across the product deliverables to give the product a coordinated appearance. Your company logos, product logos, legal notices, and graphical material should be consistent everywhere they are used. Human factors engineers also review the key technical terms of the product to make sure they are used consistently between your software, documentation, online help, quick reference cards, and marketing materials.

EXECUTION

When you've got a solid UI prototype and your project is off and running, is there anything left for the human factors engineer? Yes—plenty. The following is a description of the basic tasks the human factors engineer performs during the execution of a project:

◆ Reviewing progress of the UI at each base level and milestone.

◆ Advising on and consenting to minor UI changes.

◆ Creating (or obtaining) graphical elements for the product.

◆ Reviewing product packaging, licensing, and OOTB as previously described.

♦   Validating the software internally and externally. Although there might not be time for major changes, you might be able to make small changes. And it will certainly help you get ready for the next release.

♦ · Reviewing the software at visual freeze to make sure it meets the standards of the platform it's designed for.

COMMON PROBLEMS AND SOLUTIONS

The following are some of the typical problems and questions that surface when applying these techniques, and some solutions to those problems.

ITERATING IN CODE

One of the most common reasons why software is not delivered on time is that the team codes each iteration of the UI. If this occurs during the actual development of the software, the process of arriving at a good prototype takes dramatically longer, and the product's end date becomes completely unpredictable. In most circumstances, however, the second or third iteration is accepted whether it's good or not, just to get the product back on schedule or because that's all there is time for. I cannot overemphasize the need to iterate outside of the code as quickly as possible and to settle on a final design before committing to a schedule.

RECEIVING NO EXTERNAL INPUT

If you were to ask development teams if their UI should receive external input, you would almost always hear a resounding "yes." Yet very few product teams actually get external input—especially at the right stages—because it's very hard to get feedback on something that you haven't yet built. With the techniques presented in this chapter, you should have more success in obtaining external feedback.

STOPPING INNOVATION

One of the most common criticisms raised with the ideas presented in this chapter is that the ideas stifle innovation. What if, the question goes, after working with the product for four months I have a great new idea? Can I make changes as I see fit?

The fundamental message of this chapter is that the major elements of the UI need to be in place at the beginning of the project and should not change during the project if the original schedule is to be met. You can and should innovate, but you need to complete this innovation during the prototyping stage, which is why you need to validate and iterate quickly. By testing the prototype up front, you won't have a need for major changes later. Even if the new idea presented is a breakthrough, you still know that your current idea will satisfy your market needs and you won't have to slip your schedule. I'm not suggesting that minor changes can't be adopted during a product's development. There are often lots of little changes than can be made during development that add value and have very little cost. Many of these can and should be made because they don't jeopardize the schedule or cause significant problems.

11

Scheduling

C reating the schedule for a project can often be one of the most difficult and politically charged aspects of the entire project. Schedule the project correctly, and you'll have an effective tool to manage the project. Schedule the project poorly, however, and no matter how hard the team works, the effort will be perceived a failure if the software is delivered late. Although scheduling a project is notoriously difficult, understanding the principles of good scheduling can often make the difference between fabricating dates and developing a realistic time estimate.

In this chapter I'll detail the information you'll need to build a schedule, discuss the most important scheduling concepts, and show you how to create an accurate and realistic schedule.

PREREQUISITES

Before you build a schedule, you need to understand your project's requirements, technology, and user interface. Figure 11-1 shows the elements involved in creating a schedule. Once you understand these fundamental aspects of your project, you should have an excellent idea of what you're trying to build and how it will work.

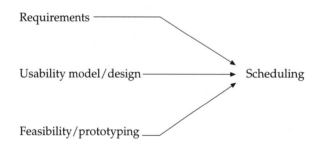

FIGURE 11-1 *Critical input to the scheduling process*

However, if you haven't defined your project's basic requirements, prototyped its biggest technical risks, or created a model of its user interface, you simply do not have enough information to create an accurate schedule. You won't be able to enumerate the tasks involved or estimate accurately how long each of them will take. Your schedule will be filled with vague tasks that are too broad to track or measure, and because of this, your schedule won't be trustworthy. It will be thrown aside at the first sign of trouble, and you'll be left without any way of managing the delivery of your project.

SCHEDULING CONCEPTS AND ISSUES

In order to create your own schedule or review one created by others, you must have a solid understanding of basic scheduling concepts. In this section, I'll discuss the fundamental concepts everyone involved in the scheduling process must understand. In addition, I'll provide an overview of the most important personnel issues involved with creating a schedule. And lastly, I'll cover some of the most common scheduling problems that development teams face.

FUNDAMENTAL CONCEPTS

The following concepts are fundamental to the creation of reliable schedules.

Balance

Maintaining a balance between the amount of work you have to do, the amount of resources you have available, and the amount of time you have to complete the project is the oldest and most important rule of scheduling. If any one of these gets out of balance—or worse, if you are given a set of constraints that cannot be balanced—you will not be able to deliver the software on time. Even if your project starts off balanced, there's a good chance it won't stay that way. Development cycles contain enough twists and turns to throw even the best schedules out of balance. The project manager must review the schedule regularly and take whatever action is required to keep the elements in balance throughout the project. I'll discuss how you can monitor your project and make changes in Chapter 12.

Tasks and Estimates

Tasks are the fundamental building blocks of a schedule; they represent the specific work that must be completed. As a general rule, it's easier to monitor the progress of smaller tasks. You can quickly find out if you're falling behind schedule when the tasks are short and precise. For example, if a task can't be completed in one or two weeks, break it up into two or more tasks. Filling your schedule with longer tasks will make it very difficult to track your progress.

When you develop a list of tasks, be sure to keep in mind the relationship of one task to others within the project. For example, know which tasks are dependent on other tasks, and schedule them in the proper order. Key features should always be completed first. You must know how long each task will take. Make an estimate—an educated guess—about how much time will be needed to complete a specific task. Because of all the work you've already done toward defining requirements, user interface, and technology implementation, your estimates should be based on solid information and be relatively easy to develop. If you can't develop solid estimates for key tasks, you probably haven't done enough investigation, prototyping, or research for the tasks.

The estimates should include all the work that must be performed to complete the tasks. For example, software engineers should provide estimates for the low-level design, implementation, debugging, and unit testing. User education engineers should estimate how much time it will take to write, review, copyedit, and proofread their own work. Although each individual creates a task estimate for his or her own work, the estimates should always be reviewed by the appropriate lead. These estimates will be used to create an overall estimate for the project, so you must be confident that the numbers have been chosen correctly.

Over time, you'll find that the accuracy of your estimates will increase, especially as you continue to work on the same product using the same technology. Be sure to review any tasks that take much longer than you expected in order to understand why the estimate was faulty.

A Complete Schedule

Don't make the mistake of scheduling just the software portion of the project— every single discipline that contributes to the project should be included in the schedule. These include:

- *Development*   The software engineering portion of the schedule should provide enough time for the product's feature development, unit testing, and debugging. Additional time should be allocated for the development team to review materials produced by the QA and user education teams, and potentially the human factors and release engineering teams as well.

- *Quality assurance*   The QA portion of the schedule should provide enough time for the development of test plans and test scripts, and for the testing of the infrastructure itself. Additional time should be allocated for integration testing of each milestone in the schedule.

- *User education*   The user education portion of the schedule should provide enough time for the development of the documentation, online help, and tutorial. Additional time should be allocated for any copyediting and proofreading that might be necessary. And don't forget technical reviews with team members.

◆   *Human factors*   The human factors portion of the schedule should provide enough time for the design and evaluation of a detailed user interface. There should also be time for an evaluation of the product's graphic material, an internal and external review of the user interface, and a documentation review. Testing the "out of the box" experience should also be included in your schedule.

◆   *Release engineering*   The release engineering portion of the schedule should provide enough time for build system development, installation development, and configuration and maintenance of the source code management system.

◆   *External dependencies*   Your schedule should also provide whatever time is necessary to account for any external dependencies that your project might have, including the delivery or use of third-party software, capital equipment availability, or even the arrival of new employees or the support of other teams.

Parallel Development

One of the important themes of this book is that running all of the aspects of a project in parallel enhances the development cycle. A good way to implement this development philosophy is through the project's schedule. Your goal is to integrate the development, QA, user education, human factors, and release engineering tasks together for the completion of specific features.

Consider this example of parallel development. Say your developers will be delivering features that correspond to the commands "Create Customer," "Modify Customer," and "Delete Customer." As soon as the features are ready and appear in the daily build, your QA team should test them and provide immediate feedback on the quality of the implementation. At the same time, your human factors teams should be evaluating the user interface to see if usability standards and implementation goals have been met. Your user education team should be finalizing their description of these features and providing feedback on quality, implementation, and integration.

Parallel development has many important benefits. First, it focuses the entire team's effort on getting a set of features implemented as soon as possible. This creates a sense of urgency, purpose, and (hopefully) early success in the project. It will also keep the team focused and in sync throughout the development process because your team will be talking about, working on, and improving the same issues at the same time. Second, because the entire team is focused on the same features, you will know much earlier if a feature is done or whether it's just coded and suffers from problems with quality, integration, or usability. You goal is to get the team to deliver solid working features as soon as possible and not be forced to revisit issues you thought had been resolved. You don't want to be surprised by quality or implementation issues on features that were supposedly finished weeks or months ago.

Build Breadth vs. Depth

When you create a schedule for your project, order the tasks so that your teams are working on the breadth of the project rather than the depth. That is to say, don't limit the focus to one part of the system to the exclusion of all the other parts. For example, if you're building a Web-based order entry application, don't schedule all the UI development tasks to be completed at the same time, followed by all the business logic tasks, followed by the entire database code. Even if you have solid design specs, scheduling your tasks one at a time will cause an integration nightmare. Instead, develop each of these systems simultaneously. Focus on the tasks that allow you to enter a simple order, store it, and display a confirmation. This approach will create your first end-to-end test and will unite the essential software subsystems of the project.

Feature Contexts

Ask a developer for a schedule of his or her tasks and you'll often hear something like, "I have to update the resource manager to include support for 32-bit identifiers, fix the PRODUCT_ID index traversal algorithm to allow duplicate entries, and rewrite error handling code to support multiple threads." Although these are all legitimate work items, you must make sure each of these tasks is in the context of a product feature or requirement. When the focus is on the feature, the developer's task becomes, for example, "support printing from the Order Entry dialog box," or "allow multiple products to be ordered in a single purchase." This narrower focus will also aid the rest of the development team because they need to understand when specific features or requirements will be available, not the specific tasks required to implement them. When your schedule clearly identifies the delivery of each feature or requirement, other team members on the project can make sure their work is completed in parallel.

PERSONNEL ISSUES

The following are some of the personnel issues involved in schedule creation.

Task Assignments

Not all developers are created equal. Some developers are skilled with user interfaces, some work on core logic. Some have more experience than others. Some will be very productive, whereas others will have average or even poor productivity. You cannot assume that people are interchangeable and that tasks can be randomly assigned. Be very careful when mapping tasks to developers, QA engineers, release engineers, and so on. Consider each person's skill, personal productivity, project experience, and work habits.

Leveling

Your goal is to assign the workload of the project as evenly as possible across the project team based on their individual capabilities. Be careful, however, that you don't assign too much of the workload to your best team members. Although they might be able to do more work than others, even they have a limit. You might also need them to help others when trouble arises.

Overhead

It's naive to assume that people will spend 100 percent of their time on their principal assignments. Every organization has overhead. Overhead includes meetings, process requirements, vacations, training, trade shows, sick days, and holidays. Even if you work 80 hours a week, you might find that 10 hours are still spent in these activities. Account for this time in your schedule. In addition to including expected events (vacations and tradeshows and the like) in the schedule, include some flextime for unexpected events like sickness and winter weather.

Slack and Critical Paths

Some tasks have slack and others are on the critical path. Tasks that have slack can be delayed without affecting the overall schedule. Tasks that are on the critical path cannot be delayed without affecting the overall schedule. When you create a schedule, you need to understand which tasks are which. You must monitor the critical path tasks closely, because any slip in their delivery will cause a corresponding slip in the end schedule or more overtime for the team. It's usually a good idea to put experienced people on critical path tasks to minimize risk to the overall project.

PITFALLS EVERY TEAM MUST AVOID

The following are some of the most common scheduling problems development teams encounter.

Target Dates vs. Committed Dates

A *target* date is a proposed date for the project's delivery. It's usually based on external market or business conditions. Although this is important information, don't simply agree to deliver a project on a target date without first creating a schedule. Use the date as a given in the scheduling equation, and then see how you can balance the features and resources to meet it. If the equation does not balance, you'll need to remove features, add resources, or some combination of both. Your ultimate goal is to build a balanced, realistic, and believable schedule that the entire team can commit to.

Once you have a solid schedule, you must make sure you secure buy-in from the team. A *committed* date is a date that the entire team agrees to. They believe it is reasonable and achievable. At this point, the development team is making a commitment to deliver the software at a specific time. With startups and large companies alike, there's a lot of people, money, and time riding on the software's timely delivery. Once the team commits to a date, it's critical that the team delivers on time and earns the credibility that comes from meeting obligations.

Schedule Ownership

All too often, development teams are told what their features are, what resources they will have, and what their dates will be. In this situation, the schedule is not owned by the development team but by the organization or person who handed down these edicts. This a formula for major problems. The team will suffer from morale problems because they will feel that they have been put in a situation that sets them up for failure. Having no sense of ownership or commitment to the project can take the heart, spirit, and enthusiasm out of a team.

Instead, the development team needs to set its own schedule—or more precisely, maintain the balance that the schedule represents. With this ownership, however, comes responsibility. If the development team owns the schedule, they must make sure they meet their delivery dates. Commitment and credibility are on the line.

Back at Work

At NuMega, there was tremendous pressure to ship products on time. Our target dates were usually key market events such as the release of Microsoft Visual Studio or the introduction of new technologies like Microsoft Windows 95, Microsoft Windows NT, or Microsoft COM. To take advantage of these events, our marketing teams developed comprehensive rollout plans that called for advertising, press briefings, analyst tours, trade shows, and sales training. Hundreds of thousands of dollars were going to be spent on these activities that were based on a software's delivery date. In addition, our sales teams and senior management were counting on a significant increase in revenue with the delivery of each product. Any delay would not only cost a lot of money and time but also delay sales opportunities and miss market momentum.

  To make sure we got the software out in a timely manner, we did our homework up front, made appropriate tradeoffs on features, time, and resources, and then built realistic schedules based on the target dates. Because of this, the schedules belonged to engineering, not marketing or senior management. But we had to commit to them—no matter what. Any mistakes in a schedule were our problem, and we were responsible for figuring out a solution without delaying the release.

Engineering Credibility

One of the biggest problems engineering groups face is the lack of credibility. When an engineering group continually misses its dates, other parts of the organization lose trust in the group. Once credibility is lost, the ability to get buy-in on schedules is compromised, judgment on project tradeoffs is questioned, and all sorts of schedule games (like false target dates or asking for more while expecting less) can creep in. But if you have a history of delivering on time, you can use this credibility to work important project issues, solicit support, and get the benefit of the doubt when you need it most.

BUILDING A GREAT SCHEDULE

Now that I've covered the basic scheduling concepts, let's focus on the details of building a great software schedule. The process has three basic steps: defining the tasks, grouping them into base levels, and grouping the base levels into project milestones.

Later in this chapter I'll provide an example of a typical schedule that describes the basic project structure you need to manage. As you will see, however, the goal is not to micromanage every detail of the project. You can't possibly know what someone will be doing on a specific date six months from now. Instead, you want a schedule that enumerates a set of well-defined deliverables that occur regularly throughout the development cycle. With this in place, you can manage the team toward each deliverable and mark and measure your progress with certainty.

TASKS

Your first step is to define all the tasks required to implement a specific feature. The total time it takes to complete these tasks is the time it will take to complete the feature. Schedule the features from the list of must-have requirements first and then move to the should-haves and could-haves. This method will help you achieve a viable release as soon as possible.

After that, schedule the QA, user education, UI, and release engineering teams' tasks. Each team will have their own set of work items based on their own project deliverables, and those tasks should be organized so they integrate with or follow closely behind the implementation of the features by the software engineers.

BASE LEVELS

Base levels define the delivery date for a group of related features. They should occur every two to three weeks. Remember, these features must be both available through the installation procedure and usable by the development team. Base levels are important short-term objectives to focus the team's attention and effort. To a large extent, nothing matters more than completing the next base level on time. If you don't hit the next base level, your project is officially behind schedule and you need to take corrective action immediately. The following are some sample base levels (from NuMega's error detection product, BoundsChecker):

◆   A source code library and nightly build are established, and a bare bones installation procedure is completed.

◆   The product hooks and logs basic memory functions.

- The product displays first memory error message using the UI prototype.

- The product successfully detects memory leak types 1 and 2.

- The product successfully detects memory leak types 3 and 4.

- The product successfully detects memory leak types 5 and 6.

- The product's real UI appears, but without print, sort, and filter support.

- Print, sort, and filter support is complete.

- The product integrates with other products in the suite.

INTERMEDIATE MILESTONES

A milestone is a group of base levels that represent the completion of a significant portion of the product. They should be evenly divided across the duration of the project. For example, if you defined four milestones for your project, each one would represent 25 percent completion. Obviously, the more complex the project, the more frequent your milestones.

Each milestone should have a stabilization and integration period, as discussed in Chapter 6. To review, this is a period of time, usually one to two weeks, during which the entire team focuses on addressing issues that have surfaced in the features that have already been implemented. These periods — during which testing is done, bugs are fixed, design and integration issues are addressed, and performance is evaluated—are critical to the project because they allow the software to stabilize. Do not move forward into new feature development until you're certain that the current features are functioning well. In addition, stabilization periods are also a great time to catch up on any work that has been delayed. This period offers the team a time for individuals or subteams to catch up with the rest of the team and get back in sync.

EXTERNAL MILESTONES

External milestones involve people or teams outside the project and mark critical points in the project. The most common external milestones include:

- *Alpha release*   This is a release with only a few critical features implemented. Alpha releases are not widely used, but they can be beneficial if you need to show progress or get feedback on critical features externally.

◆ *Beta release*   This is a release with most, if not all, of the features implemented. Beta releases are given to customers for testing and evaluation.

◆ *Release candidate (RC)*   This is a release you intend to send to manufacturing if testing is completed successfully. Release candidates are a signal that the project is nearly done and its release is imminent.

◆ *Release to manufacturing date (RTM)*   This is the date on which the production release will be sent to manufacturing (or posted to the Web, whatever the case might be).

Each external milestone requires the software to be distributed to people outside the team and even outside the company. Because of the importance of these events, you should have a stabilization period before each milestone. This allows your team to focus on quality, integration, and important fit and finish issues before the product is released. The beta release and release candidate are critically important and will be discussed in detail in Chapters 13 and 14.

AN EXAMPLE

To make sure you've understood the basics, let's walk through a detailed example, shown in Table 11-1 on page 184. Although I've simplified the project and eliminated information that would normally be included, this example should be detailed enough to show you how everything fits together. The following are the basic scheduling assumptions for this example.

◆ Scheduling principles

   ◈ Each feature has a list of engineering tasks associated with it. They are not shown in the example but could be easily listed in the document. A single task can't be any longer than two weeks; most should be one week or less. Must-have features are done first, based on requirement prioritization, and the less important features are done later.

   ◈ QA tests the features as soon as they are delivered by development. Some features will have automation, but all other features will be manually tested. The details of testing activities are described in a QA plan.

♦ User education documents features as soon as they are delivered. The documentation effort follows the features delivery as much as possible. The details of this effort are described in a user education plan.

♦ Human factors evaluates each UI feature implementation as soon as it's completed, consults on changes, and reviews the product experience as the project is developed. The details of this effort are described in the human factors plan.

♦ Release engineering will create a simple build and installation procedure immediately, and then increase the features and robustness of the build and installation procedure regularly over the course of the release. They also support the inclusion of a new feature when it is ready. These specific feature and capability improvements will be described in the release-engineering plan.

♦ Personnel

   ♦ Matt: dev lead and full time developer

   ♦ John: software engineer

   ♦ Jim: QA lead; also writes automation

   ♦ Frank: QA specialist; executes the automation and manual tests features

   ♦ Sarah: user education lead

   ♦ Kenny: human factors lead

   ♦ Bob: release engineering lead

♦ Milestones, internal and external

   ♦ There will be four bi-monthly base levels, two major milestones, two betas, one RC period, and one RTM.

   ♦ Every two base levels will form a milestone. Milestone 1 will represent half the project's completion; Milestone 2 will represent the other half.

TABLE 11-1   **A SAMPLE SCHEDULE**

Date	Goal	Dev Team		QA Team	
		Matt	*John*	*Jim*	*Frank*
Jan 01		*(White space indicates work has started on next task.)*			
Jan 08	Base level 1	F1	F2	A1	T2
Jan 15					
Jan 22	Base level 2	F3	F4	A3	T4
Jan 29		F5			
Feb 05	Milestone 1	Integration and stabilization period			
Feb 12			F6		T6
Feb 19	Base level 3	F7		A7	
Feb 26					
Mar 05	Base level 4	F8	F9	A8	T9
Mar 12					
Mar 19	Milestone 2	Integration and stabilization period			
Mar 26					
Apr 02	Base level 5	F10	F11	A10	T11
Apr 09		F12	F13	A12	T13
Apr 16	Beta 1 prep	Test for beta 1 readiness.			
Apr 23 to May 21	Beta 1	F14, F15. Fix, tune, and make minor enhancements.		A14, A15. Improve automation and test according to QA plan.	
May 21	Beta 2 prep	Test for beta 2 readiness.			
May 28 to Jun 25	Beta 2	Bug fix. Tune. Make minor enhancements.		Improve automation and test according to QA test plan.	
Jul 02	RC	Execute release candidate process.			
Jul 16	RTM	Project closure			

# (Number) = Feature identification number
F= Feature is coded and unit tested, all engineering tasks associated with it are complete.
A = Feature has test automation

User Ed Team	Usability Team	Release Engineering Team
Sarah	*Kenny*	*Bob*
		Complete simple builds and install
D1	U1	
D2	U2	
D3	U3, U4	
D4, D5	U5	Better build and install according to release engineering plan
D6		
	U7	
D7		
D8, D9	U8, U9	
Vacation		Great build and install according to release engineering plan
D10, D11	U10, U11	
D12, D13	U12, U13	Full featured install
Document activities according to doc plan	Final review: external testing, OOTB evaluation	
Document activities according to doc plan	Visual freeze	Final install

T = Feature has been manually tested
D = Feature has been documented
U = Feature has had its usability review

- Beta 1 will be one month long. Features F14 and F15 will be added during beta 1, but the rest of the time will be spent on testing, tuning, and fixing bugs. Each team member has a specific list of activities during the beta 1 time period.

- Beta 2 will have no new features. No major feature changes are allowed—just testing, tuning, and bug fixing. There is a specific list of activities for each team member during this time period.

- Release candidate

  - A release candidate will be built at the end of beta 2 if testing has been completed without major problems.

- Status meetings

  - A meeting will be scheduled every Monday to review progress. If a base level is not completed on time (or it appears that it won't be), changes required to get the project back on schedule will be made.

BETA TESTING ADDITIONS

In the example, you'll notice that two tasks are scheduled for delivery during the first beta period. Although you want to refrain from adding features—particularly important or complex features—during any beta period, it sometimes makes sense to schedule a set of low-cost and relatively low-risk features for the first beta. The longer you delay putting your product in the hands of your beta customers, the longer it will take to receive feedback on the quality and the implementation of your features. The benefits of sending your product through a beta cycle earlier can often outweigh the risks of adding minor features after the beta program has started.

Although adding a few features into the first beta period is sometimes acceptable, no new features should be scheduled for the last beta period. The final beta period is a time in which features are locked down and the team focuses on quality, performance, and fit and finish problems. Beta testing will be covered in detail in Chapter 13.

Unexpected Problems

If you have created a schedule using the principles in this chapter, you probably have planned your project as well as anyone could. However, software development is an imperfect science and problems are always nearby. You'll need to check your project's progress against your schedule regularly and compare your actual progress against each base level and milestone to see if you're on track. If you're off schedule you'll need to identify the problem, update the schedule, and hit your next base level or milestone. Sound simple? It's not—and this is where the project manager and the leads need to be on top of their game. Due to the complexity of keeping a project on schedule, I've devoted most of Part III to the subject.

Common Problems and Solutions

The following are some of the typical problems and questions that surface when applying these techniques, and some solutions to those problems.

It's Always Wrong

Creating a solid schedule takes a lot of effort, so it's easy to understand why some teams aren't willing to do it. Often, the people who are the most reluctant have tried to use schedules in the past but had to abandon them early in a project because of all of the unexpected problems that surfaced. When a schedule doesn't reflect reality, it will be largely ignored.

There's no question that scheduling is a difficult exercise, but it is an essential step. You are creating the roadmap for your project. If you need to ship on time, you must understand the work you have before you and the amount of time it will take to get it done. The techniques I have outlined in this book will make scheduling easier, more predictable, and less risky.

It's Harder Than It Looks

It seems so simple to break tasks down into time frames of one or two weeks, but it can be a real challenge. There always seems to be a three-week, four-week, or five-week task in the schedule. If you have a task that takes this long, break it down into smaller tasks. If you measure your progress in smaller time frames, you can see deviations from the plan earlier. If it's too difficult to subdivide a task, you probably don't understand it very well—a sign of significant risk. You need to prototype a solution to get a better understanding of the work.

It's Out of Sync

You need to have synchronization periods in your schedule. In addition to stabilizing the software, they provide opportunities for the rest of the project teams to catch up. You can't predict all your problems ahead of time, but you can predict that you will have some. Allocate time in your schedule for them— whatever they might be.

PART III

PROJECT EXECUTION

Staying
on Course

W ith basic planning complete, the challenge now is to turn the crank and grind out the software. Although this might seem like a mechanical process, you need to constantly monitor the progress of the project and work through the day-to-day problems. This chapter will discuss how you can effectively monitor the status of the project and take action to keep it on track.

THE AIRPLANE ANALOGY

An airplane leaves Boston bound for San Francisco. During the flight there will be countless factors that could potentially push the flight off schedule or in the wrong direction. However, the majority of direct flights arrive on time and land at the correct destination. Like an airplane, you need navigational systems and in-flight procedures to help you stay on track and on schedule. Without them you will surely be flying blind.

◆ *The flight plan*   The flight plan is designed long before takeoff. Among other things, the flight plan contains a set of steps that will take you from where you are to where you want to go (head west for 100 miles, then turn northwest at location X, then maintain course for the next 500 miles, and so on).

Similarly, because of your prototyping and usability work, you have a basic idea of what you are building and what it will look like when it's complete. Because you've done a good job with your scheduling, you have the basic steps to build the product and know when each step should be done. Part II of this book (Chapters 8–11) focused on the creation of a flight plan for your project.

◆ *Unpredictability of the trip*   Although the flight plan provides a general framework for the flight, it does not, nor can it, predict or address the enormous number of issues that can surface during the course of the trip. Wind direction, turbulence, jet stream changes, air traffic congestion, and so on can affect the flight and potentially push the plane off course and behind schedule.

Your project will also encounter thousands of issues that you can't predict or plan for. Any one of these issues could push you off course or cause a delay. And like an airplane, you need a system for responding quickly to events while you're in flight.

◆ *The navigation system*   Airplanes stay on course because they have navigational systems that take frequent measurements (every few minutes or so) of where they are, which they compare to where they want to go. Then they make small adjustments during the flight to bring the two in line. In essence, they assume they are always off course and are always trying to get back on course (Figure 12-1).

In the same way, you need a project navigational system. You need to take frequent measurements of your project and make small adjustments before you get too far off course. You need to check your progress regularly throughout the development cycle and then make the appropriate changes in a timely manner.

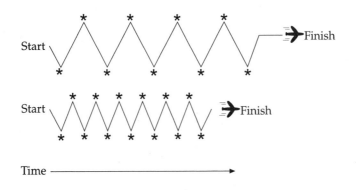

* = Measure and correct

FIGURE 12-1   *Navigating through unpredictability*

◆ *The descent*   As an airplane approaches its final destination, a set of special procedures and preparations begins—everything from receiving a runway assignment to restoring tray tables to their upright position. The flight crew has a special set of procedures to make sure that the plane lands safely exactly when and where it is supposed to. Note that the flight crew members know ahead of time what they need to do; they don't make up the procedures as the plane is heading down.

Similarly, you need to make sure you can "land" your project safely, without making any major gaffes as you head for home. You need to have a process for descending that will guide you through the final stages of your project. You want that process to be pre-defined, not made up as you're trying to land. Because of the importance of this last step, I've devoted Chapter 14 to it.

MEASURING AND MONITORING PROGRESS

As I discussed in Chapter 9, your schedule calls for specific milestones composed of specific base levels that will be available on certain dates with certain features or functionality. These will be the formal checkpoints you will use to measure your progress. If they are delivered on time and work as needed, you're on course. If they are not, you have a problem and it needs to be addressed immediately. You have the tools and processes you need to take measurements frequently because you're building every day, because your project is always installable, and because you're testing in parallel with development. And because you have a schedule that describes the delivery dates for your milestones and base levels, you know where you are supposed to be on any given date. Comparing where you are with where your schedule says you should be will let you know if you are on the right track.

Let's be clear about the importance of the above concept. If your project has just started and your first base level is due in two weeks, you must make sure you complete it on time. If you really intend to make your end dates, you must make your intermediate dates. If you have to work nights and weekends to do it, then do it. Don't wait until the end of the project to make up for lost time. You can't—it will be too late. You need to hit the deadlines right in front of you when they are due. When you make them, be sure to celebrate and share the success—it's a job well done. But if you miss them, you need to assemble the team, review what happened, and fix the problem. You also need to come up with a plan to get the project back on schedule. The entire team must take a very serious, very aggressive approach to making intermediate dates if you intend to finish the project by the date you scheduled.

You might be wondering if there is a way to know in advance whether you will hit your next base level or milestone. Although base levels and milestones are formal events and usually have hard or objective data associated with them, they are often separated by many weeks. What you need is additional instrumentation to help navigate during the periods between base levels or milestones.

The rest of this chapter will address this issue. It will provide some guidelines on how to collect soft data about your project and how to make changes in direction or speed, should they be needed. Remember, project slips don't just happen at the end of the project—they happen a little every day throughout the project.

DETERMINING THE STATUS

Getting and sharing information is key to the efficient execution of a project schedule. In this section, I'll show you the best ways to get and share status without dragging the whole project down in meetings, minutiae, and overhead. And most importantly, I'll show how you can use this information to find problems before they cause major delays or issues.

Performing Daily Builds and Smoke Tests

As I've said before, the daily builds and smoke tests will be the heartbeat of your project. Both are critical ways of determining the status of the project. If you can't build your software for days or weeks, your project is in trouble. You must have the ability to build the software in order to maintain internal consistency, integration, and visibility. If you can't build, you've lost your ability to measure the state of the project.

In addition, you must perform smoke tests. Smoke tests are critical to measuring the basic quality of the software on a regular (daily) basis. If problems are found, you must address them immediately. If you don't, it's like reading your altimeter, learning that you're quickly losing altitude, and doing nothing about it.

Meetings

Almost every group has some form of status meeting. A status meeting can be a great way to collect and communicate key information on the state of the project and keep people connected and working together. But if a status meeting is not well run, it can bore people to tears, cause a lot of frustration, and break down team cohesion. The following are some guidelines to get the most out of your status meetings:

◆ *Have a specific purpose.* The status meeting collects and shares major achievements, failures, or issues with the team. It should focus on what has and hasn't been completed. It's also a means of raising important issues that need the attention of all or many of the team members.

◆ *Ask that everyone attend.* Everyone who contributes to the creation of the project should be at the status meeting. That includes everyone I identified as part of the core team in Chapter 4: project manager, developers, and quality assurance, user education, and release engineers.

◆ *Keep the topics broad.* Status meetings often get into trouble because they are the only time when some of the team members can get together to discuss their issues. Although these issues are important and need to be resolved, the status meeting is not the time to brainstorm, work out solutions, or make major decisions. If you try to cover all this ground for everyone on your team, you're going to spend the better part of the day in meetings and waste a lot of people's time—people who only need to know what the decision is, not every detail about how it was made.

For example, does every developer need to sit through a meeting about a new online help format? Does every QA team member need to hear developers discuss the next set of changes to an API? No—if these issues can't be resolved in less than two minutes, then they need to be addressed at a separate meeting with only the appropriate people involved. The solutions that are arrived at during those separate meetings are the kind of information that should be communicated at status meetings. Don't use your team's status meetings to work out these issues.

It is also inappropriate at a status meeting to recite every single task you worked on that week. You're either on track or you're not. If you're not, then list the reasons why. Everything else is immaterial.

◆ *Keep the meetings brief.* Status meetings should be short and frequent. I'd recommend meeting once a week and giving each team member five minutes or less to explain their status within the context above. The meeting organizer, usually the project manager, has to keep the conversation focused and not allow inappropriate topics to dominate the conversation. However, any important topics raised by a team member should be added to the issues list for the project.

> ### Back at Work
>
> At NuMega, when important milestones drew near, we needed to address the latest issues and bugs as a team. To make sure we had current information, we printed out a report of these issues, listed first by priority and then by owner, and made copies for everyone at our status meetings. (Later, we replaced our printout with a laptop and network connection so we could work directly from the system.) These reviews helped mobilize our entire team to solve the important issues and bugs that were gating the progress of others or were high-risk deliverables. This intense level of communication is very important in the final stages of any milestone, beta, or release.

- *Keep a list of outstanding issues.* During the project, there will be a number of issues that surface and that will need to be addressed. In Chapter 5, I recommend tracking these issues so they are not forgotten, assigning them owners, and ensuring that the resolution is clear to all. This concept will also be useful for your status meetings. You can use the status meetings to review which issues remain open, confirm ownership, and set dates for closure. This lets everyone know that all issues will be considered and reviewed.

Managing by Walking Around

Managing by Walking Around (MBWA) is a useful concept. Although status meetings are formal, just walking around allows the project manager or leads to informally meet and discuss issues with individuals. Why is this practice so valuable?

- It shows that the project manager is involved and cares about the project. He or she isn't going to run the project behind a monitor or through numbers, charts, and figures. It makes the project manager and leads more approachable and allows information to flow quickly and easily.

- It recognizes that individuals often are not comfortable speaking up at status meetings. It's surprising what people will say one-on-one in front of the coffee machine that they would never say at the team meeting.

◆   It allows spontaneous conversation on important topics or issues, which can often bring a whole new approach to solving the problem. Great ideas don't show up every Monday at 2:00 P.M. Instead, you must encourage unstructured, unplanned, and informal communication.

Because most engineering managers were once engineers, it often goes against their grain to get out of the office and away from their computers. But it's amazing what can happen when someone walks around and asks, "How are the smoke tests working?" or "Any news on issue X?" or "Hey, are we going to make base level 2?"

◆   Good project managers and leads will be sure to spend regular time one-on-one with their team members. It doesn't have to be formal or scheduled; just a quick visit for some social chat and a work update can go a long way toward keeping people focused and working together. It's also a great way of weeding out personnel or project problems before or as they happen. If you don't want to be surprised at a status meeting—or worse, when a deliverable is due—talk frequently with each and every team member.

Sharing Information

Although the project manager and leads should be communicating effectively with each other and with the team, sharing key successes and failures with the entire group is critically important to the progress of the project. Because both success and failure are so important, let's look at each of them:

◆   *Success*   Each major success should be shared and celebrated. It's important evidence that the project is alive and doing well and that progress is being made. So when the daily build process is ready, when the initial installation procedure is ready, and when major features are checked in, be sure to send e-mail to the team and share the event with everyone. For really important milestones, be sure to share the information with the larger group—the division or even the entire company.

◆   *Failure*   Failure to deliver any portion of the product should be recognized, communicated, and resolved as soon as possible. You can't expect perfection, and you have to know that problems are going to happen. It's the team's job to find them and deal with them as soon as possible. The worst way to deal with a problem is to suppress it or deny that it exists because that neither solves the problem nor gets the project back on track.

To make sure this does not happen on your team, the project manager and team leads must be open and approachable. If the team members feel that problems or failure will not be addressed professionally, then suppression and denial of the problem will remain a lingering source of trouble.

MAKING CHANGES

There isn't a single project that won't be hit by issues or problems. Of course you hope that your navigational system will pick up any issues early, which will allow you to fix them before they become major problems. To get back on track, however, you'll need to change your course and possibly increase your speed. Let's look at both.

CHANGING COURSE

If you are contemplating changing major elements of your project—the features, technology, platforms, or schedule—be sure to consider the following guidelines. They'll keep you out of trouble and might help you make the right decisions.

◆ *Get the facts, but don't overanalyze.* All too often, major decisions are made based on impressions, emotions, or a single occurrence of a problem instead of a set of powerful facts. Before you make a change in your project, make sure there is strong evidence that a change is needed. For example, don't let an emotional statement like "the product is crashing everywhere" force you to cut half your features while you put more resources on QA. Before you make a move, find out the facts: Where is it crashing? Who is reporting the crashes? How often are they occurring? You just might find that all those crashes are related to a few common bugs that were fixed last week.

Conversely, don't get caught in the "analysis paralysis" trap. You don't want to spend weeks researching an issue only to find out that the opportunity to implement the change has passed. For example, if you've looked at making a feature change for a while but you never get enough data to decide one way or the other if it's the right way to go, make a decision now, based on what you do know.

◆ *Involve others in the discussion of the problem.* With the facts in hand, be sure to discuss the problem with the key players on the team, including development, QA, documentation, human factors, release engineering, and product management. Brainstorm ideas and discuss alternatives. If others are going to be affected, give them a chance to participate in the discussion. After a decision has been made (even if you decided to do nothing), let everyone on the team know. Keep the team informed of every significant change, the reasons for the change, and the action plan for going forward. Poor communication on project changes can cause morale problems.

◆ *Use external teams to augment development and QA.* There will be many times when you need to add something, fix something, or test something, but the team is totally absorbed and there just aren't enough free cycles. When this happens, you should consider going outside the team. If you have a technical support team, a help desk, release engineers, sales engineers, or other product team members who are available, be sure to see if they can help with the problems.

Back at Work

At NuMega, we often used our tech support team as an overflow valve for our development efforts. Our technical support team was full of bright people who needed more development experience. We were able to give them real-world experience in a variety of areas while they helped the development team stay on schedule. Of course, it often meant extra hours for the support team, but they were almost always willing to put in more time to help the development team and to pick up some experience. It opened a great career path, too. Because of the experience they gained and the work they put in, the technical support team members earned the respect of the development team and were eagerly sought for development positions. This situation also highlights another reason to hire great people in every position.

◆ *Hire consultants/contractors.* Consider hiring consultants or contractors for work that is well defined and relatively short term. Your goal is to ensure coverage of critical areas that are understaffed. Be careful about using consultants as key players or leads, however, because they are likely to leave at the end of the project.

◆ *Cut features instead of extending schedules.* Eliminating features must always be considered. If you prioritized your features and scheduled them for early delivery, you are probably in a good position to cut secondary features. Cutting secondary or tertiary features should always be considered before extending the schedule. Cutting features reduces the workload across all functional teams and ensures less risk in the schedule. Extending the schedule only increases the risk that you will miss your ship date—not a wise decision just to add features that might not make a big difference in the software's success. It's more important to ship on time than to include every secondary feature.

Ask the Right Questions

A great way to address change requests is to ask, "What if I don't?" This question is especially valuable in combatting "feature creep," which can add up to be a significant amount of work. But often, changes are made without strong business or technical justification. Although the change might be a good idea, it might not be worth the overall risk it would introduce into the project. You do want to support some level of feature improvement, but you don't want to have a project overrun by small or minor requests. Asking yourself, "What if I don't?" forces you to measure the cost of not changing in addition to the cost of changing.

The following are examples of good questions to ask the next time a feature is suggested:

◆ How much revenue will I lose if I don't do it?

◆ How many customers will benefit from this change?

◆ Will I miss or put my ship date at risk if I do it?

◆ Will I be at a competitive disadvantage if I don't do it?

◆ How much risk will I introduce to the product's quality if I do it?

◆ What is the impact on the usability, the documentation, or the build and install procedures?

This isn't to say changes shouldn't be made—just be sure that the benefit of the change far outweighs its cost.

Strive for Consensus but Make the Decision

Don't let open issues or problems fester. You must make a decision. Reaching consensus is your goal, but you must remember that it's not always going to be achieved. Also, consensus does not mean a unanimous decision—it means a majority. But if all the information and analysis is complete and consensus is still not reached—the team is split in halves or thirds—it's absolutely critical that a decision be made by the project manager or leads. Don't delay or vacillate; strong leadership is required. The team needs a decision so it can keep moving, and any delay reduces motivation and momentum. Remember, it's better to find out you made the wrong choice than to put off the decision indefinitely and never learn what the right choice would have been.

CHANGING SPEED

Despite the best intentions and planning, there are times when you'll need to pick up the pace to meet your deadlines or react to changing conditions. Although working overtime is required at most startups and is typical on most time-critical projects, there are occasions when you really need a special level of commitment—and I'm not talking about just a couple of hours a week. Before you decide to increase the pressure on your team, you need to know when it's appropriate and how to do it effectively.

When to Increase the Pressure

As the project manager or lead, it is very important to know when to ask an individual or team for extra effort. Unlike the "boy who cried wolf," however, you need to make sure that the reasons are justified and the goal is clear to everyone. The following are some of the best reasons to ask for extra effort:

♦   *To meet base levels or milestones*   If your next base level or milestone is coming up and it appears you're going to miss it, the time to start working more is now, not later. As I stated earlier, you shouldn't wait until your next deliverable to find out if there's a problem. If you think you're slipping, you need to put in extra time sooner rather than later.

♦   *To recover from a missed date*   If you missed an internal milestone, you need to make up some work. But you also need to make your next date. If you are committed to making your end date, you need to put in the extra time now.

◆ *To respond to external competitive pressures*   If there's been a significant marketing or business event, you might need to accelerate your plans in order to be successful or just to remain in business. It might be that you need to add a feature or cut the schedule by a month— either way, it will require a complete effort from the entire team.

Before asking anyone for more time, though, be sure the need for it is justified. If you are regularly asking the team to work shifts that seem like death marches or if every problem is addressed with overtime, you will drain the overall effectiveness and productivity of the team. Significant overtime can't be sustained for very long. Use it to get the project back on schedule or to react to external events, but don't make it part of your regular plan.

How to Increase the Pressure

Overtime can be required of an individual, a functional team, or the entire team. No matter who or how many people are putting in extra time, there are some basic rules to follow:

◆ *Duration*   You need to be clear on how long this time commitment will last—it shouldn't be open-ended or undefined. You should state an end goal such as a specific date or final deliverable.

◆ *Comfort*   Make the overtime enjoyable. Be sure to offer a meal for those working through dinner or snacks to those working late at night. Make sure your employees have the equipment they need to work from home if necessary. Be sure the working environment is as comfortable as possible for those who can't work at home, and make sure there is easy entrance and exit to the facility before and after regular working hours. Also consider offering services like errand running and dry-cleaning pickup to help your employees keep their energy and focus on their work.

◆ *Spirit*   When a team effort is needed, make sure there is a team commitment. Everyone stays, everyone helps, and everyone contributes. If there's no new code to write, have people work on testing. If there's nothing to test, then have them review the documentation. This shared sacrifice and shared responsibility will bring the team closer together and foster a great deal of camaraderie.

Back at Work

As a startup, there were a number of times at NuMega when we had to put in lots of hours. We often worked nights and many weekends. To make it as pleasant as possible, the daughter of a staff member would make homemade dinners. She was learning to cook and wanted to practice on us. Fortunately, she was a natural and had good supervision from her mother. We certainly had our share of pizza too, but these dinners helped break up the monotony.

When we needed to make a big push, we generally needed everyone on the team to work overtime. Everyone stayed, and everyone contributed to the overall goal of releasing the product. It was a fun time and often a social event. Although people were making sacrifices and working late, we all knew why we were there and believed we were making a difference. When the release was complete, we took the extra step of inviting family members to the release party. It was important for us to recognize the impact of overtime on our families and to try to compensate for it in some form.

◆   *Progress*   If people are putting in a lot of overtime, you want to make sure they know that they are making progress. As a project manager or lead, you need to show the team that their efforts are paying off.

◆   *Appreciation*   Recognize the team's effort and show your appreciation. You can do this at group meetings or one-on-one with outstanding individuals. You should also consider providing special t-shirts, gifts, or bonuses for remarkable efforts. Just make sure that those who are putting in the extra work know that it's appreciated. In addition, don't forget to recognize their families as well. They're being affected, too and you should find ways to recognize their sacrifice.

COMMON PROBLEMS AND SOLUTIONS

The following are some of the typical problems and questions that surface when applying these techniques, and some solutions to those problems.

KNOW WHEN YOU'RE DONE

Have you ever been asked at a status meeting, "Are you done with X?" That's actually a very vague question and could mean many different things. Does it mean the code is written and compiles? Does it mean the feature worked the couple of times you tried it? Or does it mean that the software has been thoroughly unit tested on all supported platforms and configurations? What does it mean for QA and testing or any other department? Make sure you have a definition of "done" and make sure everyone knows what it means, or you just might find people working on things that were "done" weeks ago.

BREEZE THROUGH THE SMALL STUFF

One of the cardinal sins of the execution phase is to be delayed by "small stuff." If a developer needs a larger hard drive, a technical writer needs a replacement mouse, or a QA engineer needs some ghosting software, it should be available immediately. You don't want anything small or trivial delaying your project or impairing your team's effectiveness. The project manager should be vigilant about being a lead blocker for the individual team members' issues, problems, and needs.

Back at Work

At NuMega, we worked nights and weekends as we headed into our last beta. Unfortunately, our server wasn't working along with us. It crashed randomly throughout the day, freezing the network each time it went down. We couldn't do check-ins or builds, and it was killing our productivity.

The problem went on for about two weeks, and we tried everything. We finally thought the server might be overheating because it was stored in an old closet in the center of the building (we were a startup, remember). Maybe it was not getting enough air, we thought. The next day, one of us bought a large standing fan, and we let it blow for a couple of days, but still no luck—our server continued to crash!

Finally, we wised up and decided to simply get a new server. If we had simply swapped in a new server after the first couple of days, we would have saved three weeks of worry, time, and energy.

GET BACK ON TRACK

Although most people agree that it's important to hit internal milestones, they don't put together an action plan in case target dates are missed. If something goes wrong, something must be changed to get back on track. This is another situation where the project manager earns his or her money. Be sure to track your progress against internal milestones and be sure to make the appropriate changes when you miss them.

WORK WITH HUMAN FRAILTIES

Nobody's perfect. You might find people denying that problems exist, or making comments or recommendations based on incomplete information. Pride and embarrassment can be the cause of a number of problems. Fatigue, burnout, and personal issues are factors as well. Keeping your project on track involves working with human frailties as much as it does working with technology. Learn the strengths and weakness of each member of your team, and be sure to use this knowledge to guide your decision making.

Beta Testing

B eta testing is an external software validation process. When you run a beta testing program, you send your software to a number of existing or potential customers ("beta sites") for their review, evaluation, and feedback. Your goal is to get their objective assessment of the features and quality of your software.

These beta tests provide valuable information on the readiness of your product before it is ever released to customers. For startups with limited resources, beta testing programs can be absolutely critical to success. They can allow you to leverage your QA resources in ways that would otherwise be very difficult to do. In addition to augmenting the development team's own quality effort, they can also provide objective, real-world feedback on the features of your software.

On the other hand, a poorly run beta test can be a big waste of time—not just for your development team, but for the beta testers as well. In this chapter, I'll discuss the key aspects of running a great beta program and how you can use beta testing to make your product better.

THE VALUE OF BETA TESTING PROGRAMS

Before I discuss how to run a great beta testing program, I need to discuss the value of beta testing. If you don't understand or believe in the value of beta testing, chances are you won't put in the effort and time to do it right. The following are the most significant benefits of a beta program:

◆   *Testing in the real world*   No matter how good your internal QA testing is, it would be very hard—if not impossible—to duplicate the testing performed by a large number of beta sites. If you select your beta sites correctly, they can help you test on a wide variety of platforms and in a wide variety of situations that you most likely would never have been able to cover. Because testing in beta sites involves real-world users working under real-world conditions, testers are likely to find problems you would never have been able to find by yourself.

The most important point is that good beta sites can help you verify that your software is ready to ship before you ship it. That knowledge alone is worth the effort to run a beta program.

◆ *Getting a software assessment*   A second benefit of a beta program is the feedback you receive on your software's features, performance, and user interface. Because beta sites use the product in a wide variety of conditions, they are in an excellent position to provide feedback on user needs, likes, and dislikes. In addition, you're likely to hear many new ideas from your customers. Although you don't want to change your current product significantly at this point, these ideas provide an excellent starting point for the next release.

◆ *Marketing*   An often-overlooked benefit of a beta program is the visibility and credibility it can provide for your product's marketing program. Beta sites that like the product are a great resource for press quotes and sales references. They can also serve as industry advocates for your product because they are likely to discuss, recommend, or support your product within their company or in public forums. Beta sites can help create the buzz that's so valuable when introducing a new product or release into the market.

Although beta sites can help accelerate the marketing or roll out effort, you're unlikely to experience this type of uplift with a poorly run beta program. You must be to able to communicate, respond to, and support the needs of your beta sites. You need to make the beta sites feel like extended team members. Put in the extra effort and it's more likely you'll enjoy the benefits beta sites can offer you.

◆ *Augmenting your staff*   One of the biggest benefits underlying any beta program is the staff augmentation. Whether for startups or massive development projects, beta programs can provide a significant amount of labor. This labor could cost hundreds of thousands or even millions of dollars if it were to be hired or contracted. The next time you wonder if you need a beta program, consider the following formula: multiply the number of beta sites by the number of hours each staff member spends testing your software, and multiply that by the hourly wage you would have to pay testers if you were to hire them. That amount is the value of beta testing.

The Most Common Beta Program Mistake

One of the most common mistakes of a beta program is allowing the program to drive the selection or definition of your product's core requirements. You should not use your beta program to find out what features you need in order to be successful. It's way too late for that. That should have been done as part of the market and requirements analysis (Chapter 9). If you're finding that you have completely missed the market, you should not try to jam new features into a product that's about to go out the door. You need to call time out and discuss alternatives—including starting over with a new set of requirements and a new schedule.

Remember that the purpose of a beta program is to test a product, refine its features, identify ideas for the future, and augment the marketing program. During beta, you are looking for feedback on feature implementation, enhancements, usability, and quality. These are things you have a chance of changing. You are not in a position to add major new features.

The Types of Beta Programs

A beta program is usually composed of phases. Each successive phase includes a larger group of users and a more sophisticated and stable product. Although there is no formal industry-wide definition of beta program phases, the following will give you a general idea of what each phase entails:

◆ *Beta phase 1*   At the start of beta 1, the product is between 60 and 80 percent code complete. The goal of this beta is to get the core product features to your best beta testers as soon as possible.

   For example, you might decide that you want to go to beta 1 with only the basic features complete—no print, little online help, and no sophisticated sorting, filtering, or UI features. However, the product is usable and feedback would add great value to the quality and feature-tuning effort.

   During the beta 1 testing phase, you still have time to make small but important feature changes. These changes are normal and should be expected. You want to be in a position to enhance the software based on customer input and your improved understanding of your product. However, you must be confident that the changes will not adversely affect the schedule or the quality of the product. If they will, you must weigh the cost of a schedule extension against the benefit of the new features.

◆ *Beta phase 2*   At the start of beta 2, the product is 100 percent code complete. All the features you plan to deliver in the final release of the product have been coded and are operational. Although you aren't planning to change any features, you are willing to make some changes if they are really important and are relatively low-cost and low-risk. Again, you must be confident they will not adversely affect the schedule or the quality of the product.

◆ *Beta phase 3*   At the start of beta 3, your product is at feature freeze. You are not going to change functionality or make any more changes to the feature set. This stage also implies visual freeze—the UI will not change in any significant way. The feature set is locked and the team will be focusing on improving quality, performance, and the general "spit and polish" that all great software needs to be successful. Your entire team's objective during beta 3 is to ready the product for commercial use by testing the product, fixing bugs, and finalizing the documentation.

◆ *Marketing beta*   Marketing betas are a special type of beta in which potential customers can obtain a pre-release copy of the software and evaluate it for their needs. Marketing betas are very important when the release of the product will have significant, potentially breakthrough features for customers, or when it might influence major sales opportunities for your company. In these situations, it makes sense to show customers how well the product is coming along and what it will be able to do for them when it is finished.

Because it's important to impress customers and set expectations correctly, it's a good idea to offer a marketing beta only with a late beta of the product (beta 2 or 3). That way, you can be sure the customer is seeing a high level of sophistication and quality.

Back at Work

At NuMega, when our products entered their final betas, we always sent a copy to key industry influencers. This list was composed of our business partners, key vendors, industry press, and industry analysts. As a startup, we wanted to make sure our software was freely available to anyone who could help us succeed. In a sense, it was purely a marketing beta—we had no expectation (or desire!) to be notified of bugs or issues. It was very effective in getting our name and our product into the hands of people who might help our cause.

THE ELEMENTS OF A BETA PROGRAM

In this section I'll review the important elements of a beta program and the steps you'll need to take to maximize this effort for your team.

BEGINNING A BETA PROGRAM

Before you try to recruit your first beta site, you should address some basic but important questions about the beta program.

◆   *What is the beta site profile?* Create a profile of your potential users. What skills, industry, or product experience do you need them to have? What types of technology, configurations, or platforms must they have exposure to? How much time and effort will you require from your beta sites?

◆   *What is the focus of the beta program?* Whether you are putting out a major release or a minor one, you want people to focus on the key features you've been working on. It should be clear to all your beta sites what these features are so they can direct their reviews and evaluations.

◆   *How many sites will you use?* The number of sites you use will be critical to the effectiveness of your beta program. If you have too few, you won't get very much information from your program. If you have too many, you might not be able to administrate, manage, and support all the users, which could cause frustration at your sites and cause you to lose valuable input. It's a good idea to add 30 percent more sites than you think you need to make up for the inevitable dropouts and under-performers.

Usually beta 1 uses the fewest number of sites because the product isn't quite ready for a full evaluation. Beta 1 sites are the sites that you know can work through problems and issues, and that can help debug and diagnose problems. By beta 3, however, you should have all your participating sites up and running.

◆ *How long will the beta program last?* The length of the beta program is critical as well. Although you want your beta program to be as short as possible (so you can ship the product), you don't want it to be so brief that you don't realize any of the benefits.

Back at Work

At NuMega, we had a dedicated beta manager and technical support team who could handle a fairly large beta program; we could invite about 200 beta sites. This staff provided us with ample coverage over a wide range of applications and platforms. It also ensured that we had enough coverage after some sites dropped out or did not participate. Our beta sites were a very important part of our ability to get a quality product out the door. There was no way we could have internally duplicated all the testing environments and configurations that were being used at the sites, and we appreciated their efforts tremendously.

The length of a beta program is dependent on your application, your market window, and the complexity of your release, so there is no rule that will apply well to everyone. However, we found that one month per beta (three months in total) worked extremely well for us. One month gave sufficient time for our beta testers to use the product and provide feedback. The first beta was valuable because it provided testing in parallel to our development effort. The second and third betas were devoted just to minor changes and bug fixes and were valuable to raising the quality of the product as we approached our ship date. Because we were at feature freeze by beta 2, we had about two months to improve the quality, the performance, and the "finish" of the software.

Recruiting Beta Sites

The first step in any beta program is finding and signing on beta sites. One of the most important criteria for recruiting beta sites is that they have a personal interest in the use and success of your software. As you look at the best sources for recruiting, you need to pay particular attention to their motivation.

◆ *Customers (external stake holders, internal end users)*   Your customers are often the people who are most interested in your new product development and can be terrific beta sites. They have a vested interest in seeing the product work in their environment and for their needs. Even if you don't have any customers, hopefully you have some potential customers that are keenly interested in the software you're developing.

◆ *Technical support staff*   Technical support is another great source of beta sites. Often a customer calls technical support to complain about a problem—it could be a bug or a question about how a specific feature works. If your beta software can solve a customer's problem (their bug is fixed, the product is easier to use), the customer might also be interested in being a beta site for you.

◆ *Web site visitors*   People who visit your Web site are usually interested in your product and therefore might be interested in participating in your beta programs. Be sure to allow potential users to sign up on the Web. Although you must make sure they are qualified, you should be able to generate a lot of leads this way.

◆ *Partners and alliances*   Your partners or vendors can be an excellent source of beta sites for your product. If you have business or technical relationships with other companies, sign them up. There can be a strong mutual interest in seeing your products work together.

You should have a profile of the types of sites you'd like to sign up. For example, you might want to make sure some of your sites are using a localized version of Microsoft Windows for the Japanese, Korean, or Chinese markets. Or you might want to make sure some of your sites are using SMP systems. No matter how you define your needs, when you match them up with actual beta sites, it's important that the sites provide an excellent assessment of your beta program's test coverage.

In addition, each site should sign a nondisclosure agreement (NDA) before they receive the software. The NDA will help ensure confidentiality for your software release and minimize any potential leaks to competitors.

COMMUNICATING WITH BETA SITES

Clear, regular, and honest communication between you and the beta sites is critical to the success of your beta program. You need to set expectations and address whatever issues, needs, and requests might arise, and do so in a timely manner. The following are some basic guidelines:

◆ *Set expectations.* Make it clear when the beta program will begin and when it will end, let sites know what's new in the release, and point out any specific areas that need testing or evaluation. Let sites know you would like problems reported as soon as possible and that you'd like to conduct a survey at the end of the beta program. Let them know that their feedback is valuable and that your team will fix the reported problems as soon as possible.

◆ *Broadcast major issues and solutions.* If something important doesn't work, let the beta sites know that there's a problem and that you are working toward a solution. E-mail is fine for this. But if you'd like to have more interactive conversations on issues, problems, and needs, consider a private newsgroup hosted on your Web site.

◆ *Manage issues as they arise.* Beta sites should submit their issues and problems to a dedicated (and trained) team in technical support. If you don't have a support team of any kind, someone in your development team should be designated to support the beta sites. In either case, all issues should be logged and all bugs should be acknowledged.

   You should also consider writing or, if necessary, purchasing a call-handling system for your beta issues. Call-handling systems are specifically designed to handle customers and their issues. The ability to track beta site input, communication with technical support, site location, site contact information, past bug-reporting history, call frequency, and so on can be really valuable. Call-handling systems excel at this task, but most bug tracking systems do not. If and when the users turn in a legitimate, repeatable bug, the issue can be logged in the bug tracking system.

◆   *Follow up.* For major issues or problems, it's often a good idea to have a developer follow up directly with the beta tester. This direct relationship can accelerate the resolution process and build stronger ties between the beta testers and the engineering team. It's also a great way for engineers to learn more about the customers, their problems, and their use of the software.

◆   *Address beta site problems.* Despite your best efforts, you're going to have some problems at your beta sites. Maybe your software corrupted their registry or your uninstall procedure deleted key system files. Be sure that you have the right people in place to deal with these issues appropriately.

MEASURING BETA PROGRESS

To help get the beta program off to a quick start, make sure the testers receive and install the software quickly. You can do this by posting the software on the Web or by sending it on CD-ROM. If you post it on the Web, you can monitor the number of downloads to see that it matches up with the number of beta sites. On the other hand, if you send your beta on CD-ROM, you don't have to worry about people getting the entire product.

After the beta sites have the software, make sure they are using it. It's always wise to have the beta administrator call or e-mail the sites to see that each one is up and running. It's important that there's encouragement and follow-up.

As feedback starts rolling in, be sure to check for any widespread issues that are affecting beta sites. For example, if there are installation or quality issues causing problems for a significant portion of the beta testers, you need to fix these immediately. The beta administrator or the technical support lead is in the best position to act on whatever issues might arise. These issues should be addressed as soon as possible. If they're not, the whole beta program and its value to the team could be in jeopardy.

ENDING THE BETA PROGRAM

As your beta testing cycle winds down, be sure to request that any outstanding bugs and issues be sent in. It's also a great time to send out a formal survey to the beta sites. A survey provides a formal framework for feedback on the product. It's a terrific way to find out how much the product is being used, why it's being used, and what issues or problems users are having. Too often these thoughts and ideas remain in the heads of the beta testers. Surveys are a great way to draw out those thoughts and ideas and use them to your benefit. The following are examples of some of the kinds of questions you might want to ask:

- How long have you been using the product?
- Were you able to install the product quickly and easily?
- Were you able to solve your problem or achieve your goal by using the product?
- Which feature did you appreciate most?
- Which feature was the least useful and why?
- Which feature would you like to see most in the next release?
- How could the documentation or online help be improved?
- Did the product meet your performance expectations?
- Would you use the product regularly?
- Would you support the use of the product in your group? Why or why not?
- Would you recommend it to others? Why or why not?
- Is the product ready to ship? If not, why?

Also be sure to ask your beta sites if they are willing to provide quotes or press referrals. At NuMega, we found that many of our best testimonials came from people who participated in our beta tests. We shared these testimonials with everyone in the company and, of course, with customers and the press.

> ### *Back at Work*
>
> At NuMega, when we reached the end of a beta program, we would rate the performance of each site as high, medium, or low. We'd send free products, t-shirts, and even jackets to our best beta sites. We'd send just one gift to the medium sites and we'd remove the sites that didn't participate very much. Over time, we felt we could count on our beta sites to test our new products during both beta and release candidate cycles, and to provide us with objective feedback.
>
> We once released a beta late on Friday—about 4:00 PM. We sent the e-mail to the testers and were ready to head home when one of the testers wrote back to say that he was postponing his date with his girlfriend that night just to check out our release! He wrote again later that same night to tell us the release looked good but that he wasn't done looking at it. Now that's either dedication or a personal relationship that's run its course!

Rewarding Beta Sites

With the beta program complete, it's important to review what went well and what didn't. Part of this process is to review the beta sites themselves. Beta sites that consistently provided valuable input should be recognized and rewarded. Those that didn't provide any feedback at all probably need to be dropped so that new ones can take their place.

The Beta Manager

The beta manager is the team member who is responsible for overseeing the beta testing program and managing its execution. Because beta programs are often large and complex, you probably will need a full-time person dedicated to this function. This might sound like a big commitment, but given the value that a well-run beta program can provide, you are getting more than your money's worth. The following are the basic responsibilities for the beta manager.

◆ *Establishing the purpose and goals*   The beta manager must make sure that the beta program has a purpose, customer profile, target size, and duration.

◆ *Recruiting the beta sites*   The beta manager is responsible for recruiting beta sites as described earlier. This person must make sure that there are a sufficient number of sites signed up and ready to go when the beta software is ready. Any delay in recruiting a sufficient number of beta sites will obviously reduce the amount or quality of information you receive.

◆ *Distributing the software*   The beta manager assembles and executes a plan for distributing the software to all beta sites—either online or on physical media. He or she must ensure that the software can be distributed quickly and effectively to all sites. If you decide to distribute the software online, make sure you have the communication lines and servers to support a large number of beta sites accessing your system at the same time. If you decide to distribute the software on physical media, make sure you have sufficient manufacturing capacity and can distribute the software in a timely manner.

◆ *Communicating the beta status*   The beta manager is the focal point for communicating beta status to all the beta sites. For example, the beta manager announces the start of the beta, the availability of new software, and the end of beta testing. He or she also communicates important concerns from the beta sites to the product team and vice versa. Some examples include changes in the beta program schedule, updates to the software, resolution to critical bugs, and special requests for feedback.

◆ *Managing for results*   A good beta manager can make a huge difference in the effectiveness of the beta program. As previously mentioned, the beta manager should start calling sites soon after the beta program starts, to make sure people have obtained the software and are beginning to use it. The beta manager can chart the progress of each site and make sure laggards are encouraged to install and use the software.

◆ *Ending the beta*   The beta manager must wind down the beta process without frustrating the sites that are still working with the product. The beta manager must solicit final thoughts, comments, and bug reports, and make sure they are received in a timely manner.

◆ *Rewarding beta sites*   Beta sites are extremely valuable. Good ones should be rewarded, and bad ones should be deleted. Make sure you take the time to thank your beta sites and replace those who did not participate.

COMMON PROBLEMS AND SOLUTIONS

The following are some of the typical problems and questions that surface when applying these techniques, and some solutions to those problems.

START EARLY

Recruiting takes time and so does the NDA process. Be sure to get your recruiting process started long before the beta software is ready—I'd recommend 60 to 90 days for a beta program of 200 sites.

Don't forget that beta sites are just as busy as the development team, and they can be late getting started with their evaluations. There are generally three solutions to this. First, if your product is complex or requires extensive setup resources, you can help the beta sites by sending your people to the site to help them get up and running. Second, you can anticipate that up to one-third of the sites won't start on time or won't participate at all, so you should include additional sites to compensate for this delay or lack of participation. Third, be sure to contact the sites individually, by phone if possible, to track their early progress and get an idea of their ability to participate.

TEST YOUR BETA SOFTWARE

As I discussed in Chapter 11, each beta is a major milestone in the project. As a result, you should have a stabilization and integration period for your software before you release it to your beta sites. This period—often one to two weeks—is used to test and fix bugs and to address important issues. You need to make sure your product has sufficient quality to work at your beta sites. You should consider executing the internal testing processes outlined in the next chapter before your product is released externally. Although you're not releasing your software for the final time, you can benefit from the concepts presented in that chapter when you release to beta customers.

Build a Strong Infrastructure

To run a beta program correctly, you need to have the appropriate software and hardware infrastructure. For example, you'll probably need a custom application for managing the beta sites' information, NDA statuses, participation ratings, and so on. Don't underestimate the amount of information you'll need to track and manage.

Manage Your Information

The biggest benefit of a beta program is the information you get from it. Be sure that your submission, resolution, and escalation path procedures are clear and well understood. Be sure you have dedicated and trained people to support the beta program. And be sure you stay in touch with your beta sites throughout the beta process.

Spend Enough Time

Be sure to allocate sufficient time for your beta testing. Don't think you can put a beta out on Monday and expect to be done by Friday—not if you want to get good results.

Get the Feedback

As I've said before, the value of a beta program is in the feedback. If you're not receiving a lot of feedback, you need to go out and get it. Call people. Ask them if they've installed the program and if they're having success using it. Send e-mail to make sure everyone is up and running. Send surveys to ask a wide variety of questions that can resolve issues and confirm that you're on track.

Release Candidates

You've just made the final bug fix to your project and you are now ready to make the last build of your software—the release candidate, or RC. At this point, you might think you're in the clear, but there is still a significant opportunity for major problems to arise. After all, when you release the software it is going to be used by hundreds, thousands, or even millions of people. How do you know the product is ready, or that the last set of changes didn't introduce a significant performance problem, or that important features you tested last week didn't break in the last two days? You can't take chances and hope everything is well. Pulling the software out of manufacturing or off the net after it's been publicly announced could be very costly and very embarrassing.

The release candidate process is a set of steps that systematically and objectively verify that the final build of a software product is ready for release. In this chapter, I'll cover the basic principles of the release candidate process so you can make sure your software is ready to go.

ENTRANCE CRITERIA

Before you can start the release candidate process, you must be completely finished working with the product (except for the release candidate testing activities). Despite the simplicity of this statement, there is always a strong temptation to allow some late check-ins for bugs, features, or document changes. At the point you start the release candidate process, you must maintain very strict control on any changes. Don't fool yourself into thinking you're ready when you're not. To make sure this is clear, let's go over the entrance criteria for a release candidate:

◆ *All features are complete.* Features must be 100 percent complete—all of them, no exceptions. The team should be confident that they have satisfied the release's objectives and that there are no plans to make any changes to the software if the testing process is successfully completed.

◆ *Final online user-education materials are complete.* The team has completed all online help, online documentation, readme files, and online tutorials. The material has been reviewed and is accurate and complete. The hardcopy documentation can often take an extra week, but all online material that ships with the software must be ready.

◆ *Final UI review is complete.* The team has done the UI "fit and finish" evaluation. No minor tweaks are needed before the product ships.

◆ *QA testing is complete.* The team has fully executed the test plan—unit testing, system testing, performance testing, load testing, and UI testing—and has run all automated tests. Everything passed, or at a minimum, you know what the problems are and are willing to ship with them.

◆ *Bug review is complete.* All bugs that the team intends to fix are fixed. This assumes that the team has reviewed every open bug report and made sure that the bug cannot or should not be fixed in this release.

RELEASE CANDIDATE TESTING

The release candidate represents the actual software you intend to release to customers if your last round of testing does not reveal any serious problems. Even though you have a limited amount of time, you still must test the key features of the software using the final build, which means you need to take a very aggressive approach to testing. Let's review the basic testing procedures for release candidates.

CREATE THE FINAL BUILD

After you have met the release candidate entrance criteria, you are ready for your last build. At this point, you will:

◆ Stop all check-ins to the version control system and lock the source code management system.

◆ Create one final complete build from the source code (optimizations turned on).

◆ Stop all future builds—daily builds must be turned off.

◆ Label the files in the source code management system.

◆ Notify everyone on the team that the RC software is ready!

PERFORM AUTOMATED AND MANUAL TESTS

One of the challenges of release candidates is deciding what needs to be tested on the final build. Remember, you won't be able to completely retest the product because it took months (if not years on some projects) to test. Instead, you need to have a very specific and well-defined test plan for the release candidate that can be executed in a very short amount of time. At this point, your investment in test automation will pay off again. If you've been creating automation for the key features of your product, you'll be in good shape. Your automation should cover 70, 80, or even 90 percent of what you need to test for your RC and help keep your RC phase as short as possible. If you don't have full automation, then you'll need to take the additional time to complete your testing manually. In addition to executing the automated test suite, the release candidate should focus manual testing on:

◆ Sanity installation and license testing.

◆ Core product feature testing; for example:

  ◆ Validate all key feature work.

  ◆ Touch test all major UI elements.

  ◆ Check critical links to online help.

  ◆ Validate sample programs and tutorials work.

◆ Critical performance and load testing.

◆ Other areas of specific concern to the project.

Your team should perform all of these tests internally. However, because you will soon be sending this software to customers, you should also have a small but select group of beta sites use the software and evaluate it for commercial use. This external validation can provide objective data on the readiness of the release. In the final days of any release there's often a lot of pressure on key team members, and external input can provide the unbiased assessment they need to make good decisions. After all, if your software can't be used successfully in a dozen customer sites before you ship it, how can you expect it to be used successfully in a hundred or a thousand sites after you ship?

The beta administrator is in a good position to select a subset of your best customers for this process. To be good sites, they must agree to use the software in real-world situations, be able to work within your RC testing time frame, and provide you with the information you need should problems occur. During the RC phase, you need to be in almost daily contact with these sites to make sure they are progressing and providing either positive or negative feedback. Because the relationship with RC sites is often more intense than with other beta sites, you usually have fewer RC sites than beta sites.

Back at Work

At NuMega, we asked only our best beta testers to participate in our release candidate phase. After our internal testing was completed, we'd send the software to RC sites and ask them to give us a "go" or "no go" decision within three to five days. Our beta administrator would stay in contact with the release candidate sites, and if any problems arose, the testers would get priority support—often directly from the engineers themselves. With the intense pressure to release a product, customer feedback can be either very reassuring or very alarming. After the product shipped, we'd often send our RC sites a complimentary copy of the product and development team t-shirts to thank them for their effort.

LAND YOUR PROJECT SAFELY

If you recall the airplane analogy from Chapter 12, you know that your goal is to gradually bring your project to a graceful landing over a short period of time. Just as an airplane's crew does, you need a set of predefined procedures that will guide you through this landing process. It's finally time to put your tray tables up and pull your seatbacks to their upright position.

Because the release candidate process is a critical time for the project, it requires open and clear communication on project status—both success and failure. It also requires quick but solid decisions on key issues, fixes, risks, and alternatives. To meet these needs, create a "descent team" composed of leaders from all functional teams, including:

- Development
- Quality assurance
- User education
- Human factors
- Release engineering
- Technical support
- Product management
- Beta administration

Back at Work

At NuMega, before we started having descent meetings, we had a lot of problems in the final stages of our releases. The problematic areas included current release status, issue escalation, issue ownership, testing coordination, rumor control, decision making, and team-wide communication. Problems became particularly acute as the teams grew larger and we started shipping suites instead of just individual products. At times, we must have looked like the Three Stooges! Fortunately, we came up with the descent process described in this chapter, and it largely solved our endgame execution problems.

The idea is to create a war room—a single place where issues can be raised, reviewed, and discussed. Descent meetings should occur every day at the same time in the same room. With this preplanned approach, everyone will have a formal and organized platform to report on status or outstanding issues. As the final testing is occurring and external customer feedback is coming in, there's often much information that can and should be shared. Even if there are no issues or problems, it's still a good idea to get everyone together so this good news is communicated. Finally, if a critical decision has to be made immediately, simply call an emergency descent meeting.

When Things Go Wrong, Think

As the final testing is being performed, the quality team, support team, beta administrator, engineers, or any team member might discover a real problem. This issue should be brought to the descent meeting where the descent team can:

- *Clarify the problem.* First make sure the problem is real. Then investigate the nature and impact of the problem, find out if it is repeatable, and look into which platforms or how many platforms are affected.

- *Assess the impact of any fix or change.* Determine first if a fix is possible, and then look at the scope and magnitude of the change to the software.

- *Decide whether to rebuild the software.* Weigh the costs of fixing vs. the costs of not fixing the problem at hand. Is the problem significant enough to justify the time it will take to fix it, especially if fixing it means delaying the release of the product?

If you rebuild, you should rename the release candidate using the naming scheme RCn+1, where *n* is the number of the release candidates built so far. Make sure everyone knows the new build number of the latest release candidate.

◆ *Execute the release candidate testing cycle again if necessary.* If the fix is perfectly isolated, you can retest only that portion of the product, but you must still perform installation testing again.

These are very important decisions and you need to make sure that you have the right people involved from the different functional teams. Because you are resolving these problems at the descent meeting with all the key players present, you can be assured you will have good input, solid support, and clear communication of the decisions.

When Things Go Well, Sign Off

If the release candidate testing is completed successfully, it is time for sign-off. Final sign-off on the product should largely be a formality because the successful execution of the release candidate process defines when a project is "done." However, sign-off ensures that everyone who contributed to the product and everyone who needs to support it is ready to stand behind it. Sign-off should be made by:

◆ *Engineering* Each team—development, QA, user education, human factors, and release engineering—signs off together. Their sign-off indicates that the functional teams that contributed to the actual bits are ready to let the project go. In the NuMega model, the project manager has the final responsibility for the readiness of the product based on the input and advice of the team. Engineering signs off first—if they don't, the product doesn't go any further.

◆ *Product management* The product management team's sign-off indicates that the feature implementation is market-worthy and that the licensing, pricing, sales training, manufacturing, and marketing plans are in place and are ready to go.

◆ *Technical support* The technical support team's sign-off on the product indicates that there are no critical issues outstanding and that the team is ready to support the product when it hits the street.

◆ *Customers* The customers' sign-off indicates that the product is ready for use in their production or commercial environments.

When It's Done, Ship It

With sign-off complete, you are ready to ship your product! Congratulations! But before you think you're done (and you're really close now), be sure to read the next chapter, "Project Closure."

COMMON PROBLEMS AND SOLUTIONS

The following are some of the typical problems and questions that surface when applying these techniques, and some solutions to those problems.

LEADERSHIP

One of the most common problems in smoothly completing a project is the lack of execution leadership or discipline in the final stages of the project. This is when the project manager earns his or her keep. There must be one person whose job is to ensure that the software gets out the door. Running an efficient descent process is not easy. You might need to keep the team for the weekend to rerun tests or deny a last set of really cool changes because they are too risky. Take whatever steps are needed to get the job done right.

COMMUNICATION

With all the activities and associated pressures of getting a product out the door, communication can often break down and rumors and allegations can heat up. Be sure you have a descent process to guide the product to closure, to communicate status, and to address any issues as they surface.

RESPONSIBILITY

With all the communication and decision making involved in producing software, it's important to have one designated responsible individual on each of the teams involved in the release candidate phase. The last thing you want is for responsibilities to be juggled among a different set of people over time. You want people who can consistently speak for and commit their teams to the decisions that are made.

TEST PLAN

As I mentioned previously, you need to have a specific testing plan for the release candidate. You can't test everything—there just isn't enough time. You need to focus on the most critical areas of a product. But many teams don't have a clear idea of what they need to do and how they are going to do it. Think your endgame testing needs through before you enter the release candidate phase.

AUTOMATION

If you don't have sufficient test automation, you're in trouble. The ability to automatically test the key features of a product on the final build and any necessary subsequent builds is crucial to fully validating the product in a timely manner. You don't want to spend weeks manually testing the product for each RC.

15

Project Closure

The project has finally ended. You shipped! So you must be done, right? No, not yet. Shipping a project is more than just getting it out the door and going home. A lot of time, effort, and sacrifice has been made, and it's critical that there be proper closure for all the team members. Skipping this step misses a great opportunity to reward and recognize the team for their contributions and prepare them for the next project.

Why Is It Important?

Closure brings final resolution to a project team's efforts. It also helps team members feel that the project was important and that their contribution and sacrifices were recognized and valued. Too often, the conclusion of the project is anticlimactic and can lead to bewilderment and even work-related depression. People wonder if their effort, overtime, and sleepless nights were worth the effort. Your team members might ask themselves, "Was I noticed?" "Was it worth it?" and more importantly, "Will I do it again?" Proper closure addresses these questions. Proper closure should:

- Communicate to everyone that the project is over—it's shipped.
- Recognize individual achievement, contribution, and sacrifice.
- Recognize the team's overall effort and performance.
- Help team members to look at and learn from any mistakes.
- Address immediate personnel or project issues.
- Start the preparation for the next project.

How Do I Do It?

Bringing closure to a project is not hard, but there are many tasks that need to be performed. The following is an explanation of the tasks that the project manager and the leadership team should perform.

Delivery of the Bits

The transfer of a software product from a product team to the world should be a public event. There's no more definitive closure to a project than the transfer of ownership from the team to the customer. The entire team should witness it. It's a clear and a memorable moment for everyone involved.

For example, if you are releasing the software to a manufacturing organization, you could have a representative from the manufacturing team receive the CDs from the project manager at a small hand-off ceremony at work. If you are sending your bits electronically, you could gather the team together to witness the final press of the Enter key. In any event, collect the team together and make sure everyone knows that you've shipped.

Of course, a small speech is probably in order. It's always fun to ask people to remember the more difficult parts of the project and how the team worked together to solve them. It's also fun to talk about some of the more comical parts of the project and wonder how you were ever lucky enough to survive them!

Compare having closure with the alternative. When team members have to wonder whether the project has shipped, or find out after the fact that they were not included in the delivery, they won't feel like a part of the team. They'll feel instead like a cog that has performed a duty in a larger machine but was not an integral part of a greater team effort. This shouldn't happen, and it doesn't have to.

FINAL E-MAIL

With a larger or geographically diverse team, it can be difficult to get everyone together. In these cases, it's common to send a final project-related e-mail. The e-mail will let everyone know, simultaneously and equally, that the project is over and that the team achieved its goal. This message can serve as a catalyst for post-release celebrations.

POST-RELEASE CELEBRATIONS

One of the greatest moments after the release of a software product is the post-release celebration. The feeling of completion followed by a celebration is terrific. The further apart these moments are, however, the less of an impact the celebration can have. After you release your software, consider any one of the following:

- Pop open a bottle of champagne.
- Serve ice cream sundaes at work.
- Take the team to lunch.
- Take everyone out to the movies.
- Have a cookout at someone's house.
- Go bowling.

Whatever you decide to do, make sure that everyone can participate. Some types of activities, like paintball or mountain biking, might not be desirable to everyone.

PUBLIC RECOGNITION

Public recognition, when used wisely, can be a very powerful way to thank teams and individuals for their exceptional performance. Public recognition can be done on a team level, a larger group level, or a company level. But regardless of the size of the group, there are some basic rules that you need to follow:

- *Recognize significant achievement.* You want to reward efforts that went above and beyond the call of duty.

- *Recognize excellence from all functional areas.* Don't recognize people in only one department.

- *Explain achievements to the audience.* Don't assume everyone knows what occurred. Tell the audience a story about problems that arose and how the actions of the team or an individual solved them.

- *Provide some type of memento.* A plaque or cash award will make the recognition really special.

Back at Work

At NuMega, we had company meetings almost every month. The entire company would attend and listen to updates from the different teams. At the conclusion of the meetings, we would give out the "Save The Company" award. This award recognized an employee's superior contribution on a critical problem, an employee's handling of a difficult situation, or a big win from the sales team. We always described the person's or team's actions in story form so that everyone understood why this was important and why the recognition was deserved. As a memento, we gave out "I Saved the Company" baseball caps, which the employee or team could proudly wear or display in their office.

PRIVATE RECOGNITION

Private recognition is also a very effective way of demonstrating that an individual's contribution to a project is valued. In fact, heartfelt private recognition often means more to people than any form of public recognition.

Private recognition is usually a meeting in which the project manager or lead openly and honestly thanks a person for his or her contribution to the project. Simple statements like, "I'm really glad you tested those other platforms at the end of the project—if we hadn't found that bug, we would have had to recall the product," can mean a lot to someone who made the extra effort and solved a key problem. It also lets an employee know that management knows what happened and that they appreciate it.

Private recognition can also be extended through e-mail. A kind thank you note can be very important to those who receive it. Hopefully, you've all received unexpected kudos at one time or another and know the feeling.

CASH, STOCK, AND GIFTS

Another way to give recognition comes in the form of awards. Nothing underlines or backs up a statement of appreciation like receiving a cash bonus or stock options. When given, these awards show that good work is noticed, and more importantly, that it is rewarded. Often, people are willing to work even harder when they know that management values, recognizes, and rewards excellence.

Although cash and stock are perhaps the most desirable, they are not always possible or available. In this event, consider some other type of award. A gift certificate or extra time off can convey a sincere "thank you" too.

PICTURES AND EASTER EGGS

As I've said from the beginning of this book, a software project is a team effort. What better way to emphasize this point than to take the team's picture at the end of the release? Give each team member a copy and keep one framed and on display in a public area at work—ideally on a wall dedicated to the company's releases. Posting these pictures shows everyone that there is a history of appreciating and recognizing teamwork in your company. And over time, it's great to look back and see who worked on which releases.

Additionally, many teams like to put *Easter eggs* in their products. Easter eggs are hidden commands or menus combined with mouse clicks that invoke a hidden display that contains the names and sometimes the pictures of the team. They are like the credits at the end of a movie.

Back at Work

At NuMega, our BoundsChecker team put an Easter egg in our product. For those of you who have a copy, you can see it by going to the Help/About dialog box. Place the mouse pointer on the checkered product icon, and then press the Shift key and click the right mouse button three times.

WHAT'S NEXT?

When recognition is complete, it's time to turn your attention to preparing for the next project. This is an important time, although it escapes many people's attention. It is one of the best times to learn from past mistakes and to prepare for what will come next.

LEARNING FROM THE PAST

To prepare for the future, you need to understand what happened in the past. What went well? What didn't go well? What is the biggest change you should make for your next project? What product, process, technology, or piece of equipment were you screaming for months ago and want to make sure you get in place now?

The classic way to review the project is through a postmortem meeting. This meeting typically brings the team together shortly after the release to brainstorm and share different points of view about what went well and what didn't. The idea is not to make accusations or to find personal faults, but to work together to build a list of lessons learned and action items for the next project. This meeting can be a terrific way of building momentum for change.

INVESTING IN INFRASTRUCTURE

The days and weeks after a release are also a great time to invest in your infrastructure—processes, automation, equipment, and tools. As you know, it can be very difficult to make significant changes in these areas during a project. Let's look at each one:

- *Processes*   Take a good look at your processes for daily builds, smoke tests, requirements, scheduling, usability, and descent. Are you communicating well with the team? Are your plans and templates adequate for your project? Do any of these areas need improvement?

- *Automation*   Teams often find that their release engineering automation or test bed automation was insufficient for their purpose. This is the ideal time to improve your automation and to catch up before the next project starts.

- *Equipment*   Take this opportunity to get the hardware you need for your upcoming projects.

- *Tools*   As I said in Chapter 5, changing your source code management or bug tracking tools in the middle of a release is usually a mistake and will always require more time if it is attempted then. But when a project is over, take some time to evaluate new versions of your existing tools and to update what you've got.

INVESTING IN PEOPLE

Investing in your people is as important as investing in your infrastructure. Let's look at some specific ways to do this:

- *Performance reviews*   Give performance reviews at the end of a project. Although most companies link reviews to an employee's hire date, giving reviews to each team member at the end of a project while his or her contribution is fresh in your memory provides time to fix or address problems before the next project starts.

- *Cross training*   Consider swapping responsibilities between team members. It's very important to cross-train team members on different parts of a system. You don't want to be dependent on just one person for entire portions of a system. Cross training provides more flexibility in the schedule and gives each member of your team a firmer grasp on numerous aspects of the project.

- *Training*   This is a great time for people to get more training. With a project behind them, team members can focus on learning a new technology or catching up on all that's happened since the last time they shipped.

- *Time off*   In almost all cases, vacation time is recommended for all team members. This is a great time to devote to family and personal interests. People are willing to work hard and put in a lot of overtime if they know that they'll have some down time after a product has shipped.

    For people who have worked especially hard for extended periods of time, a leave of absence or a sabbatical might be in order. You must guard against burnout of your key inner circle contributors, and letting them take some extended time off is a great way to address this issue. Your goal is to keep people engaged and energetic so they are able to deliver maximum performance over time.

At a startup, working overtime is necessary and expected, so the need for longer periods away from work is even more acute over the long run. At NuMega, after five years of employment we were allowed a one-month paid sabbatical. We were all glad to know that all of our extra hours would be recognized over time. Thankfully, more companies are recognizing the need for extended vacations and the value they can bring to both the employee and the company over time.

COMMON PROBLEMS AND SOLUTIONS

The following are some of the typical problems and questions that surface when applying these techniques, and some solutions to those problems.

THAT EMPTY FEELING

Some people can feel a little bit empty or let down after a project has shipped. They feel their contribution and effort were not worth the personal cost and sacrifices. And then they find themselves doing it all over again with little chance of addressing real project-wide problems or conquering new personal challenges. To avoid this problem, be sure to bring proper closure to the project, recognize key contributions, have postmortem meetings, conduct performance reviews, swap assignments, and give people time off.

BURNOUT

Burnout is the most severe case of "that empty feeling." People who get burned out have no energy or interest in their project or even their profession. Burnout occurs over time and can be a real problem after it hits. The main purpose of this chapter is to discuss steps you can take to prevent the problem from happening rather than dealing with it after it occurs.

NO FOLLOW THROUGH

Many of the practices mentioned in this chapter are probably not new ideas, but far too often, teams fail to take the need for these activities seriously enough. Put a specific plan in place to make sure each of these closure activities is performed and don't work on the next project until you've completed the current one.

INDEX

A

accuracy of UI in early development, 174
adaptability, 9
airplane analogy, 206
alpha release, 195
alternating development leads, 161
analyzing performance, 93
applied research. *See* research
assessment grids, 149
assumptions about technology, 158, 164
attitude, 6
    problems caused by ranking, 65
automation, improving, 253
automation engineers, 53
automation testing, 93
    benefits of, 102
    of builds, 128
    importance of, 122, 134
    of release candidates, 239, 245
    of software configurations, 117
    test beds, 52–53, 104
    of UI elements, why not to use, 104

B

backing up, 79
balancing skill sets and
    functional expertise, 59

base levels, 194
    getting back on track after missing, 220
    working overtime to meet, 216
behavior, changes in, 66
benefits, how to distribute, 64
beta program administrators, 58
beta releases, 196
beta sites
    communicating with, 229–30
    feedback from, 235
    newsgroups for, 229
    non-disclosure agreements with, 229
    partners as, 228
    recruiting, 228, 234
    and release candidate testing, 240
    rewarding, 232
    sending software to, 230
    sources for, 228
    surveying, 231
    testimonials from, 231
beta testing, 222. *See also* release candidate
      testing
    adding features during, 200
    benefits of, 113, 222
    call-handling systems for, 229
    common mistakes, 224
    ending, 231
    feedback from, 235
    information management, 235
    infrastructure for, 235
    manager, 232

257

retaining employees, 34
  common problems, 38
  effective techniques, 36
  identifying problems by using
    ranking, 65
reviewing résumés, 22
rewards, 251
risks, identifying, 166
roles and responsibilities, 59. *See also
  individual job titles*
RTM date, 196

S

salaries, 64
samples of work, 31
scalability of projects, 59–60
schedules
  balancing with resources, 187
  base levels, 194, 216, 220
  for beta testing, 200
  breadth vs. depth, 190
  building, 193
  changing pace, 216
  committed dates, 192
  convincing team to create, 201
  creating, 158
  example of, 196
  inclusiveness, 188
  master, 47
  measuring progress (*see* checkpoints)
  meeting, 208, 215
  order of, 194
  overhead, allowing for, 191
  ownership of, 192
  and parallel testing, 189
  problems, allocating time for, 202
  project manager's responsibility for, 47
  realistic, 192
  sickness, allowing for, 191
  sub-dividing, 201
  synchronization periods, 202
  target dates, 192
  task assignment, 191
  working overtime to meet, 216–18

scheduling
  development, 188
  human factors, 189
  QA, 188
  UI, importance to, 174
scripting tools, 93
sell message, 31
service packs, 124
sickness, scheduling for, 191
simultaneous editing of files, 77
skill sets, balancing with functional
    expertise, 59
small stuff, 219
smoke testing, 107, 128
SoftICE, 93
software
  configurations, testing, 117
  features (*see* features)
  feedback on (*see* beta testing; release
    candidate testing)
  installation (*see* installation procedures)
  licensing prototypes, 181
  presentation, 181
  prototypes (*see* prototypes)
  releasing (*see* release candidate testing)
  requirements (*see* software
    requirements)
  testing (*see* testing)
  usability, 181
software development
  and research, 160
  scheduling, 188
software development teams
  augmenting with external teams, 214
  communication between, 55
  communication with project
    managers, 45
  external teams, augmenting with, 214
  importance of proper staffing, 42
  interaction with customers, 69
  interaction with project managers, 43
  introducing processes to, 71
  leadership by project manager, 48
  leads (*see* development leads)
  linking together, 48
  processes, introducing to, 71

team
  creation, 60
  history, as indicator of success, 105
  pictures, after release, 251
teams, descent, 241–42
technical leads, 150
technical support, responsibility for, 58
technical support engineers
  as developers, 214
  release candidate sign-off, 243
  roles and responsibilities, 57
technology
  anticipating changes in, 149
  assumptions about, 158, 164
  evaluating, 163–64
  prototyping with, 167
  understanding, 163
templates
  for Environment folder structure, 83
  for Imports folder structure, 84
  of product structure, 82
test automation tools, 93
test beds, automating, responsibility for,
    52–53, 104
test labs, 120, 128
test plans, 52–53
testability, 104
testers. *See* QA engineers
testimonials from beta sites, 231
testing
  as part of culture, 115
  assessing results of, 112
  automation (*see* automation testing)
  automation test beds, responsibility for
    writing, 52–53, 104
  automation tools, 93
  beta (*see* beta testing; beta sites)
  for beta release, 234
  builds, 128
  by internally using products, 115
  check-in, 106
  completing, 110
  configuration (*see* configuration testing)
  culture and, 115
  dependence on UI, 174

testing, *continued*
  developers' responsibilities during,
    101, 115–16
  equipment necessary for, 118
  example of, 112
  features, 50, 108
  in parallel (*see* parallel testing)
  installation procedures, 108-9
  integration (*see* integration and
    stabilization testing)
  labs, 120
  lack of execution/commitment
    during, 122
  manual, 118
  performance/load, 111
  plan, developing, 113
  preparation for, 121
  QA responsibilities during, 116
  real-world (*see* beta testing; release
    candidate testing)
  release candidate (*see* beta testing;
    release candidate testing)
  responsibility for, 50, 101, 114
  smoke, 107, 128
  stabilization/integration (*see* integration
    and stabilization testing)
  touch, 105
  UI dependence, 174
  UI prototypes, 178
  what, when, and how, 106
  when to fix bugs during, 112
time, not enough, 19, 64
time off, 254
time-based prioritization, 88
tools, 94
touch testing, 105
tracking bugs. *See* issue and problem
    management software
tracking changes to files. *See* source code
    management systems
trade shows, 17
training, 253
trends, researching, 162
TrueCoverage, 93
TrueTime, 93
turnover, 39

U

UI
accuracy of, 174
documentation, importance to, 174
external input for, 183
key tasks for, 173, 176
prototypes (*see* UI prototypes)
review, final (*see* beta testing; release candidate testing)
scheduling, importance to, 174
specifications, developing prototypes with, 178
testing, 104, 174
UI prototypes, 172
benefits of, 158, 172
developing, 166, 175–76
documenting, 167
evaluating, 167
existing technology and, 167
external input for, 183
and human factors engineers, 180
for installation procedures, 180
iteration of, 150, 179
licensing, 181
modeling, 167
paper, 176
RAD tools, creating with, 178
responsibility for defining, 180
software requirements, defining with, 147
specifications, creating with, 178
stifling innovation with, 184
testing, 178
UI testing, 104
unit tests, including in source code management systems, 78
usability, 181
user education, scheduling, 188
user education leads, 53
user interface. *See* UI
user problems, identifying, 142

V

values for corporate culture, 68
vendors as beta testers, 228
verifying fixed bugs, 89, 92
version control, 76
virus-checking software on build machines, 128
vision statements, 141
Visual Slick Edit, 96
Visual Source Safe. *See* Microsoft Visual Source Safe
Visual Test, 94
VSS. *See* Microsoft Visual Source Safe

W

Web sites
important components of, 14
posting jobs on, 13
finding candidates with, 13
visitors, as beta testers, 228
winging it, 168
work samples, 31
working overtime, 19, 216–18
working with limited time/resources, 19, 64
workplace
extracurricular activities, 36
social environment of, 35
writing effective job descriptions, 12

ED SULLIVAN

An 18-year veteran of the software industry, Ed Sullivan received his bachelor's degree in computer science with high honors from Merrimack College. Later, he earned a master's degree in computer science from Boston University.

Ed worked for Digital Equipment Corporation at their Spitbrook corporate software engineering facility in Nashua, New Hampshire for 11 years. He held a wide variety of engineering and managerial positions involving the development of software tools for the validation of the VAX/VMS operating system. Eventually he joined Digital's consulting division and led the development and deployment of a set of customized software products for a $6 million laptop-based customer engagement management system.

In 1994, Ed joined a small startup called NuMega Technologies, Inc. Initially he served as both the development manager and product-marketing manager for their BoundsChecker C/C++ error detection product. As the development manager, Ed owned the overall delivery of four product releases during a critical time in NuMega's history. As the first product-marketing manager, he played a significant role in developing the product's positioning, messaging, advertising, and rollout strategies.

Later, as Director of Engineering for NuMega, Ed guided their entrance into the then-emerging Visual Basic, Java, and Web development markets. He drove the product strategy and implementation for eight different products in four unique market segments. During his tenure as development manager and director, NuMega's products won many industry awards, including a Technical Excellence award and an Editor's Choice award from *PC Magazine*, six Jolt Cola awards, and several Reader's Choice awards.

In 1999, Compuware Corporation acquired NuMega Technologies. As the current Development Center Director of the NuMega Lab of Compuware, Ed manages over 160 people and oversees products that generate more than $40 million in annual sales.

The manuscript for this book was prepared and submitted to Microsoft Press in electronic form. Text files were prepared using Microsoft Word 2000. Editing, production, and graphic services for this book were provided by Online Training Solutions, Inc. (OTSI). Graphics were created with Macromedia FreeHand 8. Pages were composed using Adobe PageMaker 6.5 for Windows, with text and display type in Palatino.

Cover Designer
Greg Hickman, Microsoft Press

Illustrator
Damon Studio, Microsoft Press

Project Editors
Joyce Cox and Gabrielle Nonast, Online Training Solutions, Inc.

Copy Editor
Nancy Depper, Online Training Solutions, Inc.

Proofreader
Jan Bednarczuk, Online Training Solutions, Inc.

Graphic Artist
Leslie Eliel, Online Training Solutions, Inc.

Compositors
R.J. Cadranell and Leslie Eliel, Online Training Solutions, Inc.

Contact Online Training Solutions, Inc. at:
◆ E-mail: *joanp@otsiweb.com*
◆ Web site: *www.otsiweb.com*

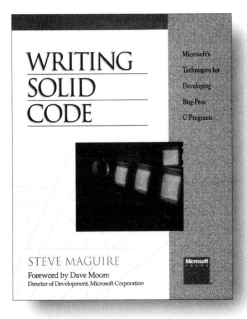

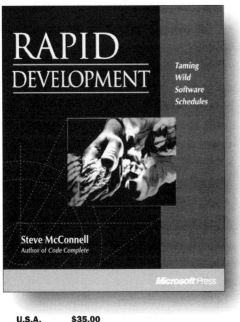

Enable
seamless
business-to-business
data exchange
with XML, BizTalk™, and SOAP.

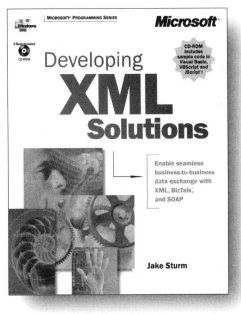

U.S.A. **$49.99**
U.K. £32.99 [V.A.T. included]
Canada $72.99
ISBN: 0-7356-0796-6

Extensible Markup Language (XML) has emerged as the most important format for moving data over the Web with the greatest variety of tools and platforms. DEVELOPING XML SOLUTIONS provides expert insights and practical guidance on how to use XML to access, manipulate, and exchange data among enterprise systems. This comprehensive developer's guidebook examines the newest XML-related technologies for data exchange, and it shows how XML fits into the Microsoft® DNA architecture for distributed computing. It also explores real-world technical examples in the Microsoft Visual Basic® programming language, Microsoft Visual Basic Scripting Edition (VBScript), and Microsoft JScript® to show how to create specific XML-enabled solutions for client/server and n-tier systems, and other scenarios.

mspress.microsoft.com

For information about Microsoft Press®
products, visit our Web site at
mspress.microsoft.com

Microsoft®